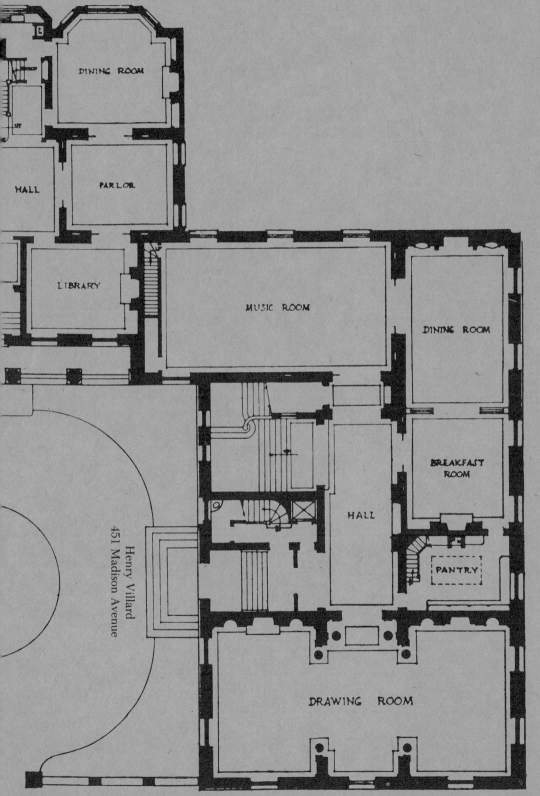

Artemas H. Holmes
453 Madison Avenue

DINING ROOM

HALL

PARLOR

LIBRARY

MUSIC ROOM

DINING ROOM

BREAKFAST
ROOM

HALL

PANTRY

Henry Villard
451 Madison Avenue

DRAWING ROOM

Madison Avenue

THE VILLARD HOUSES

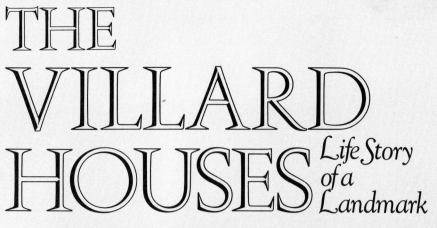

THE
VILLARD
HOUSES *Life Story of a Landmark*

William C. Shopsin, A.I.A.
Mosette Glaser Broderick
Foreword by Henry-Russell Hitchcock
Introduction by Brendan Gill
Prologue by Sarah Bradford Landau

in cooperation with The Municipal Art Society of New York

For Doris C. Freedman

First published in 1980 by The Viking Press
625 Madison Avenue, New York, N.Y. 10022
Published simultaneously in Canada by
Penguin Books Canada Limited

Library of Congress Cataloging in Publication Data
Shopsin, William C
    The Villard houses.
    (A Studio book)
    Includes bibliographical references and index.
    1. New York (City)—Dwellings.   2. Eclecticism
in architecture—New York (City)   3. Historic
buildings—New York (City)—Remodeling for other
use.   4. Villard, Henry, 1835–1900—Homes—
New York (City)   I. Broderick, Mosette Glaser,
joint author.   II. Title.
NA7238.N6S54   728.3′12′09741   80–5357
ISBN 0–670–74685–1

Printed in the United States of America

Set in Caledonia
Index prepared by Lionel Dean

Title page: *Early view of the Villard houses, taken from
the east end of St. Patrick's Cathedral. The photograph was
found in the attic of one of the houses.*

he Municipal Art Society of New York wishes to express its thanks to the authors of this book: to Mosette Glaser Broderick for the early architectural and social history of the Villard houses, and to William C. Shopsin, AIA, for the recent history and the preservation story.

he authors wish to thank the many people whose kind assistance and support made the book possible. First among them are Margot Wellington, Executive Director; Henry Ng, Deputy Director; and Mary C. Black and Hayward Cirker, members of the Board of The Municipal Art Society. Their initial commitment and continued confidence were a source of strength throughout the preparation of this book.

Special votes of gratitude are due to Brendan Gill, whose readiness to come to the aid of preservation causes is well known, but whose gracious encouragement to new authors should be equally celebrated; to Professor Sarah Bradford Landau and Professor Henry-Russell Hitchcock for their constant interest, guidance, and inspiration; and to all three for their invaluable contributions to this book.

A great debt is owed to those who generously shared both their memories of the houses and photographs from their personal collections: Mr. and Mrs. John G. Winslow, Clarence F. Michalis, and Mrs. Leighton Lobdell. A special note of gratitude to Geoffrey Platt and R. J. Linder for both pictures and information.

Many thanks also to J. Richardson Dilworth, Mrs. Margaret Drummond-Wolfe, James Mimnaugh, Ogden Reid, Whitelaw Reid, and Mrs. Lawrence Grant White. Their recollections were a source of enlightenment about many details of the history of the houses.

For their kind patience and assistance, thanks to Adolf K. Placzek, Herbert Mitchell, Charling Fagan, Janet Parks, and the staff of the Avery Architectural and Fine Arts Library of Columbia University; Esther Brumberg, Photo Archivist, and Steven Miller, Curator of Paintings, Prints, and Photographs at the Museum of the City of New York; Dr. James J. Heslin, Director, Wendy Shadwell, Curator of Prints, and the librarians of the New-York Historical Society; John H. Dryfhout, Superintendent of The Saint-Gaudens National Historical Site, Cornish, New Hampshire; Jeanie James-Rengstorff, Associate Curator of the Archives Division of The Metropolitan Museum of Art; Margaret Tuft and the Landmarks Preservation Commission of the City of New York; The New York Landmarks Conservancy (in particular Alexandra Cushing Howard, who prepared the National Register Nomination for the Conservancy); Monsignor Joseph P. Murphy, Chancellor, and The Archdiocese of New York; Paul Palmer of the Columbiana Collection, Columbia University; Martha Ramsey of the Houghton Library, Harvard University; Virginia Barton of the Dobbs Ferry Historical Society, and Jean Jacques Strayer of the Darien, Connecticut, Public Library.

Appreciation and thanks also to Harmon Goldstone, F.A.I.A., Wayne Harrison, Carol Herselle Krinsky, Catha Grace Rambusch, Robin Julie Sand, and Gavin Stamp.

And finally, special thanks to Barbara Burn, Director of Studio Books, Gael Towey Dillon, Associate Art Director and designer of the book, and Mary Velthoven, Senior Editor, without whose patience and understanding this book would not have become a reality.

Contents

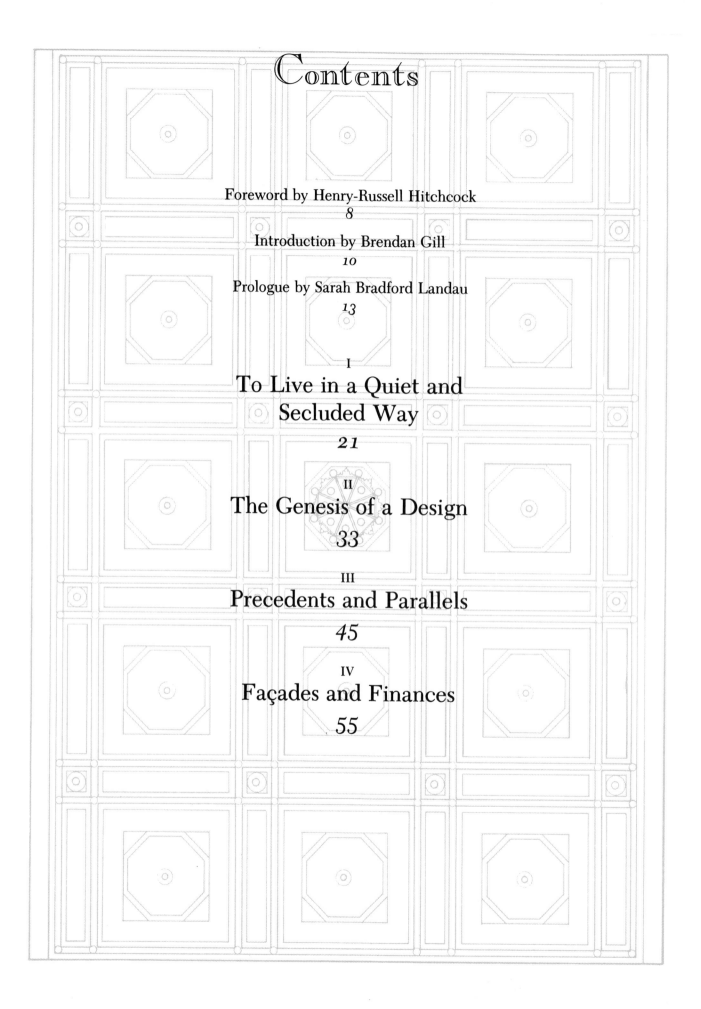

Foreword by Henry-Russell Hitchcock
8

Introduction by Brendan Gill
10

Prologue by Sarah Bradford Landau
13

I
To Live in a Quiet and Secluded Way
21

II
The Genesis of a Design
33

III
Precedents and Parallels
45

IV
Façades and Finances
55

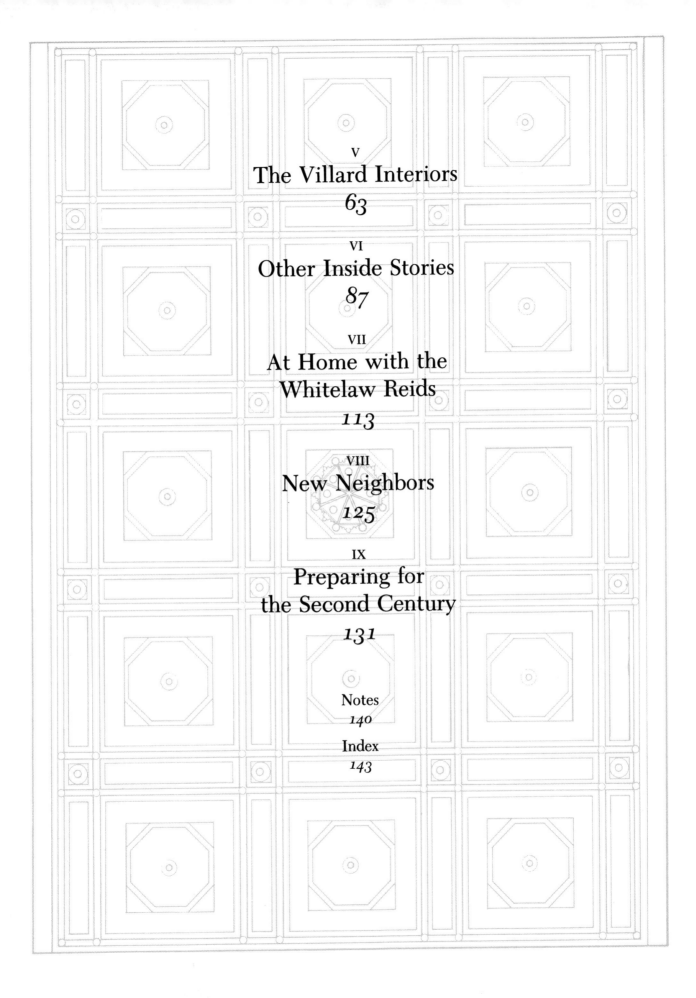

V

The Villard Interiors

63

VI

Other Inside Stories

87

VII

**At Home with the
Whitelaw Reids**

113

VIII

New Neighbors

125

IX

**Preparing for
the Second Century**

131

Notes
140

Index
143

Foreword

uring the later 1970s in New York City more architectural works of distinction were preserved than were built new. They ranged in size and prominence from Cass Gilbert's Woolworth Building of 1913—the tallest building in the world when it was erected—to modest rows of small houses in various "historic districts." The most important of these architectural works is the group of Villard houses on Madison Avenue; they were always all but unique.

From the first, contemporary critics recognized the special importance of this palazzo in the New York scene, and historians have generally recognized that in the Villard houses McKim, Mead & White (and more specifically their designer, Joseph M. Wells) initiated a movement in American architecture that may be called the "return to order"—something that neither the Tiffany house, commissioned at the same time, nor the then newly completed Vanderbilt houses of G. B. Post and Richard M. Hunt, can be properly considered to have done.

With the current reassessment of the architecture of the eastern United States in the last decades of the nineteenth century, the historic importance of the Villard group has been repeatedly emphasized anew. In its day the group had several rivals in New York, of which the finest, the De Vinne Press building (1885–1886) on Lafayette Street, by Babb, Cook & Willard, happily survives, although the equally notable and more influential Produce Exchange (1881–1884), by G. B. Post, has gone.

Today it is the intrinsic quality of the Villard houses that should be emphasized rather than their historical significance. The imitation of Italian Renaissance palaces had been no novelty in America since the 1840s, but except for the Atheneum by John Notman, in Philadelphia, the quality of these forgotten monuments was never in a class with that of the Villard houses. It is not the use of elements borrowed from Roman palaces of the sixteenth century, but the way these elements were combined that was significant in the early 1880s. The result is no less worthy of comparison with the Italian originals than is Sir Charles Barry's Reform Club in London of nearly a half century earlier. There, the handling of the attic story has to many critics seemed superior to Michelangelo's treatment of the top story of the Farnese Palace in Rome.

It is not easy to define the architectural quality of any period, but it is particularly difficult for the later nineteenth century, when architects, especially in America, often leaned heavily on the Renaissance past. Not even McKim, Mead & White, later lacking the continuing assistance of Wells, were able to reach the same level of quality in their largest and most prominent Renaissance work in New York, the University Club on Fifth Avenue, concerning which Le Corbusier once said that he preferred the Renaissance as imitated in New York to the original in Florence.

In America, clients have not always received the credit that is their due from posterity; happily, that has not been the case with the Villard houses. Although it was Whitelaw Reid who took on the responsibility and brought Villard's house to completion after construction was interrupted in 1883, one must recognize, in the group of houses as designed, the European taste of Villard. In addition to the basic plan-concept, there must be credited to him the insistence on the use of brownstone rather than the light-colored stone the architects preferred. In this extraordinary monument, the details owe much to Joseph M. Wells' borrowings from the Cancelleria and the Farnese Palace in Rome, but support for this choice must have been strongly backed by Villard so that, for the resultant quality, he shares the credit with the firm of McKim, Mead & White and more specifically with Wells.

It is in the ashlar masonry and the superb scaling and integration of such features as were borrowed from Renaissance Rome—the cornice, the quoins on the corners, the windows in the main story, the arcade at the rear of the court—that a timeless quality is present, as it is also in the exquisite elaboration of those interiors for which Stanford White was particularly responsible. One has only to compare the Villard houses, with their restrained dignity and their superb handling of the familiar New York brownstone, with the W. K. and Cornelius Vanderbilt houses to realize that a new standard of distinction—maintained, alas, only rarely afterward—was achieved in the former, in strong contrast to the latter mansions, which were little more than overblown examples of contemporary Late Victorian house design, elaborated with a profusion of French, rather than Italian, sixteenth-century detail.

The rescue of the Villard houses is one of the major achievements of the rising support for the preservation of New York's architecture, which, happily, is sure to continue increasing.

Henry-Russell Hitchcock

Introduction

n his Foreword, Professor Hitchcock does well to call attention to the exceptionally close relationship that existed between McKim, Mead & White, the architects of the Villard houses, and Henry Villard, the railroad magnate who commissioned the project. I. M. Pei has said, in respect to his design for the East Building of the National Gallery of Art, in Washington, D.C., that if a structure gains the approbation of history, at least forty per cent of the credit should go to the client. (In Pei's case, the client was Paul Mellon, whose architectural connoisseurship is demonstrated by the fact that he also commissioned the Yale Center for British Studies, designed by Louis Kahn.) We have no way of knowing whether McKim, Mead & White would have agreed with Pei's generous estimate of a client's value, but it appears that with them, as with most architects, a correlation can be found between the distinction of a given building and the distinction of the person for whom it was designed.

At first glance, such a correlation appears so obvious as scarcely to be worth commenting on, but at second glance one sees that it isn't obvious at all—indeed, it begins to assume an air of the agreeably mysterious. For in the difficult process by which a building comes into existence, the presence of a strong-minded architect and a strong-minded client might be expected to lead as readily to failure as to success. Every step in the preparation of a design is at once intimate and alienating; the disparity between what is desired and what is feasible is hard to bridge, and first-rate people, whether architects or clients, are rarely of a douce and conciliatory nature. Throughout history, the relationship of architect and client has been apt to oscillate between admiration and antagonism, with trust and suspicion alternately filling the charged air above the smudged, inky plans, and often enough projects have remained on paper, forever unbuilt, because what had begun as a hoped-for collaboration ended in an abrupt collision. Among the clients of McKim, Mead & White were some of the most powerful—and stubborn and opinionated—figures in American life, and it says much for the grace and forensic skill of the partners that they not only got along well with the oligarchs but persuaded them to commission structures, both domestic and institutional, that were far more elegant (to say nothing of far more expensive) than they had anticipated building.

For several decades, McKim, Mead & White was a firm so fashionable and therefore so busy that it amounted to a kind of factory, as well as a forcing-shed for young architects who were subsequently to make careers under their own names. Much of the work done by the firm at its factory-worst has mercifully fallen out of the ken of history; the McKim, Mead & White buildings that we find remarkable today are nearly without exception buildings commissioned by remarkable men, among them Charles Tiffany, J. Pierpont Morgan, W. C. Whitney, Robert Goelet, and, not least, Henry Villard. It is pleasant to speculate upon the different personalities of these clients and to attempt to measure the degree of influence they may have had upon the aesthetic intentions of McKim, Mead & White. Morgan, for example, was known for his quick temper and imperious ways. He complained once to his friend Henry Walters about the amount of trouble that McKim had given him over the design of his library, and it was to avoid just such trouble that Walters offered the task of designing his new art gallery in Baltimore not to some celebrated and perhaps stiff-necked architect but to young William Adams Delano, who at the time hadn't designed so much as a doghouse. Where in the serene and exquisite spaces of the J. Pierpont Morgan Library lie any evidences of the Morgan temper, the McKim trouble-making? Perhaps in the course of construction they were silently transmuted into lapis lazuli.

Of all the clients of McKim, Mead & White, none comes down to us more vividly over a period of nearly a hundred years than Henry Villard. Plainly, he was a charmer from birth, and there was little that anyone ever felt inclined to refuse him. A Bavarian of old family and excellent education, he came to this country in part seeking adventure and in part perhaps to remove himself from the shadow of his august father. By his mid-twenties, he was already a celebrated journalist; in his thirties, he was a highly successful promoter and builder of railroads, and in 1881, at the age of forty-six, he was at the height of his financial success and therefore in a position to think about building a substantial city dwelling for himself and his family. Being related by marriage to McKim, whom he had earlier employed in the development of a country seat in Dobbs Ferry, Villard was quick to offer the commission for the project to McKim, Mead & White.

In glancing back upon that critical opening moment in the design process, one ought to bear in mind how young the architects were. William Rutherford Mead, who managed the office and kept his kitelike partners from tangling in midair and, as Mead said, "making damned fools of themselves," was thirty-five, McKim was thirty-four, and White was twenty-eight. (Also twenty-eight was Joseph Wells, the architect in the firm who is generally given credit for having designed the accurate Renaissance façade of the Villard Houses.) The firm itself was scarcely two years old and thus at the very beginning of its fame. Its motto was characteristic of the high spirits of the partners: *"Vogue la galère!"*, which can be freely translated as "Here goes!" Their senior by over a decade and intensely European in attitude, Villard was far more sophisticated than his architects and almost certainly had a far greater knowledge of what was of interest in the urban architecture then being practiced throughout the Continent. He was familiar at first hand with the block-long, multi-story apartment houses being constructed in Munich, Vienna, and Berlin, as well as with the age-old French *hôtel particulier* and Italian *palazzo:* imposing piles of stone that looked from the outside as if they were a single grand family dwelling but that contained within their walls half a dozen or more separate households.

In bringing the European notion of a private palace to New York, Villard hoped that he would be furnishing a model for the improvement of our domestic architecture, with its conventionally narrow and gloomy row houses giving way at last to sunny open courtyards and green gardens. The Villard model, brought to reality in the crisp, self-confident designs of McKim, Mead & White, was much admired but not, alas, much imitated. Though its appearance had a strong effect upon the architectural fashions of the time, its usefulness as a solution to a problem in urban design was negligible. Most nineteenth-century millionaires courted fame, not anonymity; what they considered to be an ideal personal monument wasn't a fraction of a house on Madison Avenue but the whole of a house on Fifth Avenue. We are fortunate that, after innumerable vicissitudes, the Villard Houses continue to stand. As the text that follows makes evident, after almost a century we have much to learn from the close collaboration of Henry Villard and his band of gifted young architects. *"Vogue la galère!"* is a glad shout that never altogether dies away.

Brendan Gill

Le Roy Place, built 1826–1827 and since demolished. Engraving after an 1831 drawing by A. J. Davis. (The New-York Historical Society.) Right: Nos. 4–13 of The Row, Washington Square North, built 1832–1833. Nos. 7–13 have been renovated as an apartment house. (Photograph by Sarah Bradford Landau.)

Prologue

The Villard Houses and the New York Row House

n choosing to build adjoining houses for himself and his business associates, Henry Villard was adhering to a venerable Anglo-American form of city residence, the terrace house or row house. The Villard houses are nonfreestanding, private houses built in keeping with the nineteenth-century ideal of urban life. Yet few would dream of referring to them as row houses, for the term "row house" connotes speculative building, standardization, and, frequently, narrow widths—none of which characterizes the Villard houses. Even so, the houses do share party walls and are vertical units, and they compare significantly to the finest of New York City's historic rows.

The century-long existence of New York as a city of private row houses was rooted in an English tradition going back to Inigo Jones's Covent Garden in London, begun in 1631. After the great fire of 1666, London was gradually developed and expanded into a city of secluded residential squares lined with eighteenth- and nineteenth-century Georgian terrace houses. America's great eastern cities adopted the English row house—colonial Philadelphia, Federal Boston, New York, Baltimore, and others. In New York the row house supplied the need for private houses in the form of multiple units which could be easily fitted into the grid pattern. The size of the New York lot, 25 by 100 feet, as established with the grid plan in 1811, was scaled to the dimensions of a row house two rooms deep with a generous rear yard.

Most of the city's early row houses were modest brick dwellings planned so simply that any mason or carpenter could design them with the help of a pattern book. In the 1820s and 1830s the length of a row built all at once was rarely longer than two or three houses, but there were a few long rows built, some of them with impressive granite or marble fronts. Said to have been the "first planned monumental blockfront in the city,"[1] Le Roy Place consisted of two granite-fronted rows which faced each other across Bleecker Street near Broadway. They were erected in the late 1820s by builder Isaac G. Pearson. On one side of the street the group of late Federal-style houses were united as a long palatial front having a center and wings and set back behind 10-foot-deep gardens. As in the case of the Villard houses, the individual units were subordinated to the whole block. The prototypes for the arrangement of the Le Roy Place houses were late eighteenth-century English terraces.

The finest of the city's early rows and one of the few built in Manhattan with a mews lane is located on Washington Square North east of Fifth Avenue. The Row, as it was called, indicating its exclusiveness, was originally comprised of thirteen brick-fronted and marble-trimmed Greek Revival houses erected in 1832 and 1833. Although the houses presented a homogeneous group, having been built according to a uniform design, their details varied; for example, some doorways are flanked by Ionic columns, and others by Doric columns. The raised parlor floors are entered from high stoops under which there are servants' entrances to the ground or basement stories. High stoops were an identifying feature of the New York row house all through the nineteenth century, and although only low stoops are in evidence, the Villard houses were also constructed on the high-stoop plan with raised parlor floors. The leases for the Washington Square North lots, drawn up by Sailors' Snug Harbor, which still owns the land, restricted building to "a good and substantial dwelling house, of the width of said lot. . . ."[2] The Villard houses, too, comply with restrictions in the deed which required either private houses or French flats—a term then used to give distinction to apartment houses. As a rare example of controlled planning of their period, The Row provided an early precedent for Henry Villard.

Still another exceptional row of houses having a uniform façade is La Grange Terrace, usually designated as Colonnade Row, on Lafayette Street. A two-story Corinthian colonnade unites the group as one magnificently colonnaded block, but unfortunately only four of the original nine marble-fronted houses survive. Built by speculator Seth Geer at the same time The Row was going up, they were the homes of prominent and wealthy men, among them John Jacob Astor, Jr., and Edwin D. Morgan. A watercolor by Alexander Jackson Davis proposes what may be an alternative scheme for La Grange Terrace—two pilastraded terraces with rooftop pergolas facing each other across a fence-enclosed green and built back into the depth of the block rather than along the line

Watercolor rendering by A. J. Davis possibly of an alternative scheme for La Grange Terrace (1832–1833), known as Colonnade Row, at 428–434 Lafayette Street. (The Metropolitan Museum of Art, Harris Brisbane Dick Fund, 1924.)

La Grange Terrace (1832–1833), known as Colonnade Row, as it was ca. 1900. Only the four houses at the right, 428–434 Lafayette Street, are still standing. Left: The House of Mansions, built 1856 by A. J. Davis and now demolished. Across the avenue is the Croton Reservoir, on the site where the New York Public Library now stands. (Museum of the City of New York.)

Grand Army Plaza, Fifth Avenue between 58th and 60th streets, ca. 1895. At the extreme right is a corner of the Cornelius Vanderbilt mansion. Facing it is Mary Mason Jones's mansard-roofed Marble Row, designed by Robert Mook and built 1867–ca. 1873. All the buildings seen in the picture have since been replaced. (Byron Collection, Museum of the City of New York.) Left: Marble Row in 1892.

of the street. Davis even offers two different treatments of the block ends. In respect to its ingenuity and attempt to break with the standard relationship of housefronts to street—there are more commonplace brick houses at either side and in the background—Davis's extraordinary scheme seems a prediction of the unusual arrangement of the Villard houses.

Davis was the architect of a group of exceptionally picturesque houses known collectively as the House of Mansions. These once occupied the block front running from 41st to 42nd streets opposite the Croton Reservoir (the site of the New York Public Library). Their brick fronts were treated as a medieval castle, and the houses were set back from the street behind deep front gardens. The builder, George Higgins, advertised the group as "altogether unique in its character and plan, the eleven buildings being combined as in one palace or massive edifice, thereby exhibiting a unity of mass not before attempted though often desired by critics."[3] Each occupant of the House of Mansions could boast of living in his own castle, just as Villard and his friends could imagine that each of them lived in a palace. Davis's houses did not have high stoops but were English basement houses. Never widely used in New York, the English basement house enjoyed a brief vogue in the 1850s. Such houses were entered on the ground floor, and from there one climbed the staircase to the parlor floor. Completed in 1856, the group failed to sell, and in 1859 the Rutgers Female School bought the northern portion of the row for institutional use. By 1891 the row was but a ghost of its former self, having succumbed to the commercialization of Fifth Avenue.

Two other impressive rows might have influenced Villard and his architects—the famous Marble Row, begun in 1867 and completed in the early 1870s on the east side of Fifth Avenue between 57th and 58th streets, and the Colford Jones Block, built from 1869 to 1870 and located farther south on the same side of Fifth Avenue between 55th and 56th streets. Marble Row was designed by Robert Mook for Mary Mason Jones, the aunt of Edith Wharton and the model for the redoubtable Mrs. Manson Mingott in *The Age of Innocence*. First a large and lavishly appointed house was built for Mrs. Jones herself at the 57th Street corner, and then the others followed until there were seven in all. The Villard houses were constructed in similar order, with Villard's own house completed first. Edith Wharton wrote of Mrs. Mingott that she "put the crowning touch to her audacities by building a large house of pale cream-colored stone (when brown sandstone seemed as much the only wear as a frock-coat in the afternoon) in an inaccessible wilderness near Central Park." With their mansard roofs, Parisian motifs, and gleaming marble fronts, the row of "Second Empire" houses was a Fifth Avenue showplace. Rebecca Jones, sister of Mary Mason Jones, built the Colford Jones Block to the design of the Danish-born Detlef Lienau, who was trained in Paris. The row of eight houses, faced with light Ohio stone, was more elegantly high-style than Marble Row, being modeled after the contemporary French apartment house. According to Ellen Kramer, the two blocks "set a standard of luxury unequalled in New York until the 1880's."[4] Both were monumental blocks in the grand tradition, and both were highly successful enterprises.

Brownstone came into fashion for housefronts in the late 1840s and remained popular through the 1870s. Easily and inexpensively obtainable from New Jersey or Connecticut, it could be cut into thin blocks and assembled as a smooth, nearly seamless front. It was well suited to the *palazzo* mode, originated by Charles Barry in his Travellers and Reform clubs in London and accepted in New York by the early 1850s for the row-house front. To New Yorkers, brownstone seemed a more dignified material than brick: it made a row of houses look instantly old and tastefully designed, and it conferred status as well as equality with one's neighbors—qualities Villard may have desired. Although by no means obsolete, brownstone was no longer high-style when Villard commissioned his houses. For example, the Tiffany house, also designed by McKim, Mead & White and under construction during the same years as the Villard houses, combined rock-faced bluestone and tan Roman brick in its façades. The Dakota apartment house and its companion row houses on West

73rd Street, designed by Henry J. Hardenbergh and built by Edward S. Clark concurrently with the Villard houses, are faced with yellowish or red brick and trimmed in brownstone and olive-colored sandstone. People had become tired of the monotonous rows of brownstones on the East Side. The showiest of the new mansions were not brownstone: George B. Post's early French Renaissance-styled Cornelius Vanderbilt house, begun in 1879 and completed in 1882 on the west side of Fifth Avenue at 58th Street, was faced in pressed red brick trimmed with light stone, and Richard Morris Hunt's François I William K. Vanderbilt house, begun a few months later in 1879 and completed in 1881 on Fifth Avenue at the corner of 52nd Street, had gray Indiana limestone façades. These ostentatiously large houses may have seemed a vulgar display of wealth to Villard, as they did to others at the time.

Henry Villard was perhaps influenced in his choice of brownstone by the pair of mansions built from 1879 to 1881 by William H. Vanderbilt on the west side of Fifth Avenue between 51st and 52nd streets just south of the William K. Vanderbilt château. Designed by John B. Snook, assisted by Charles B. Atwood, then with the Herter Brothers firm, these boxlike houses of *Néo-Grec* inspiration were connected by a one-story solarium. One can well imagine Villard asking his architects to give him something similar. Other notable and well-to-do New Yorkers acquired brownstone-faced houses in the early 1880s. Samuel J. Tilden, a former governor of New York State, had Vaux & Radford remodel a pair of houses on Gramercy Park South for him during the years 1881–1884[5] as one house with a brownstone front in the polychromatic High Victorian Gothic style. In 1880 banker J. Pierpont Morgan bought a brownstone mansion, built about 1853, on the corner of Madison Avenue and 36th Street, and in 1881 Wall Street financier Jay Gould purchased a mansarded brownstone mansion on the corner of 47th Street and Fifth Avenue.[6] In requesting brownstone of his architects, Villard may have been conservative and even old-fashioned, but he was in the best of company.

In respect to their arrangement and plans, the Villard houses are not typical New York row houses. Instead of relating to the street line, they form a U-shaped block around a courtyard in the manner of the French *hôtel*. Apparently the architects and Villard wished to complement the clergy houses, to which the projecting wings respond, and the east end of St. Patrick's Cathedral (as it was before the Lady Chapel was added in 1906) across the street. Together the opposing buildings formed a square bisected by Madison Avenue. Villard's mansion is almost entirely independent of the other houses in the group, and the three houses in the north wing were each of different dimensions and plan. Only the Adams and Holmes houses in the center can justifiably be considered row houses in plan—originally they were mirror images. The Smith and the second Fahnestock houses had rather unusual interior arrangements, though the rooms were laid out one behind the other as in row houses. The Harris C. Fahnestock house at the end of the north block had mansionlike dimensions even before the adjoining house was annexed in 1922 and is more deserving of the label "town house" than "row house."

Unlike all the rows discussed, the individual Villard houses cannot be distinguished unless one is familiar with the plan. Two of them, suppressed in the interests of perfect symmetry, are undetectable from the main courtyard front. Their entrances (formerly high stoop) are on 51st Street. Although quoins above the ends of the loggia, aligned with the chimneys on the party walls, represent the divisions between the center pair of houses and the houses on either side, they also serve to deceive one into thinking that the adjoining wings represent two mansions of equal size. Nowhere else can the party walls be located from the outside. The recessed twin doors of the center houses are apparent, but the arcade—clearly devised for the purpose—effectively joins these houses as a single unit and obscures the view of the doors from the street. Well disguised by the brownstone shell of McKim, Mead & White's brilliantly conceived neo-Renaissance *palazzo*, the Villard houses are at once the most deceptive and the most monumental of the city's rows of houses.

Sarah Bradford Landau

The Colford Jones block,
designed by Detlef Lienau
and built 1869–1870 on Fifth
Avenue between 55th and
56th streets. (Lienau
Collection, Avery Library.)
Below: Vanderbilt residences
on Fifth Avenue. At left are
the mansions of William H.
Vanderbilt and his daughters,
Mrs. Elliott Shepard and Mrs.
William D. Sloane. At right is
the William K. Vanderbilt
house. (Museum of the City
of New York.)

Henry Villard. Below: *The Gustav Hilgard family home at Zweibrücken, where Villard lived in his youth.* (Houghton Library, Harvard University.)

Residence of the Gustav Hilgard family at Zweibrücken in the Palatinate, in which Henry Villard lived until he was forbidden to continue his schooling because he refused to prepare for the prize in the revolution of 1848 and was sent to boarding school in France. His father lived in this house from 1843 until 185-. It was still standing as shown in 1931.

To Live in a Quiet and Secluded Way

pulent and awe-inspiring, the brownstone palace on Madison Avenue between 50th and 51st streets known as the Villard houses would seem the very epitome of the grandeur of New York in the 1880s. But this is not one house, it is six, and they and the man whose name they bear are in many ways uncharacteristic of their time.

To begin with, although Henry Villard was a highly successful railroad enterpreneur, his personal fortune was nowhere near that of the Vanderbilts or Jay Gould, who were also creating magnificent houses for themselves at this time. The site on which Villard was to build was just as large as theirs, but Madison Avenue was then unfashionable and nonresidential. Finally, Villard's architects produced what was (for New York at this time) a unique house, the first in the city in the post–Civil War period to be styled in the manner of the Roman palaces of the High Renaissance. This Roman Renaissance style was quite unlike the *Néo-Grec* design of Charles B. Atwood (1849–1895) and John B. Snook (1815–1901) for the William H. Vanderbilt house, the Loire Valley château style of Richard Morris Hunt's design for William Kissam Vanderbilt or George B. Post's house for Cornelius Vanderbilt, all of them on fashionable Fifth Avenue.

But uncharacteristic as they are, the Villard houses are the only New York City town houses built for the railroad barons of the last century to have survived to this day. A look at Villard's career provides a unique basis for an understanding of the houses and their occupants, for everyone connected with the houses was linked to Villard through journalism, the abolitionist cause, or the railroads.

The child who was to become known as Henry Villard was born in Speyer in Rhenish Bavaria in 1835 and baptized Ferdinand Heinrich Gustav Hilgard. The family later moved to Zweibrücken, where he spent his youth. At the age of eighteen, with no money, connections, or knowledge of the English language, he departed for America, changing his name from Hilgard to Villard as he left European soil. It has been variously reported that he took the name of a French schoolmate, that he did not want to embarrass the family name if he became a failure, or that he sought to avoid being returned home for military service. In his memoirs, Villard gave no reason for the change. It was an era of massive German immigration into the United States, and he may have chosen a French-sounding name to enhance his image.

Like many young men, Henry Villard was something of an adventurer and unsure of what he wanted to do. Upon arriving in America, he traveled to the German-settled areas in what was then known as the West and in 1854 settled in Illinois. There he met a cousin, Gustav Koerner, who had established a legal practice in southern Illinois and had become closely connected with another young lawyer, Abraham Lincoln. Koerner had exchanged his European political concerns for enthusiasm for the freedom from slavery of American blacks. He soon succeeded in making his young cousin an acolyte for the cause.

Villard, who needed a livelihood and had always enjoyed writing, began to submit columns to the German-language newspapers. In 1856–1857 he was editor of the Racine (Wisconsin) *Volksblatt*, and within five years of his arrival in America he was reporting the Lincoln-Douglas debates for the *Staats-Zeitung*, a daily paper published in New York. Early in his career as a journalist, he had encountered Lincoln at a deserted railway station, and when a sudden thunderstorm forced them to take refuge in an empty freight car, they squatted on the floor and talked of politics, their origins, and religion.

By 1860, when he was assigned to cover both the Republican National Convention in Chicago for the Cincinnati *Commercial* and the election, Villard's career was on sure footing. He became the Springfield, Illinois, correspondent for the New York *Herald* and was assigned to cover Lincoln's activities during the months after his election. During the Civil War, from 1861 to 1863, he reported from the battlefield first for the *Commercial* and later for the *Herald*. In 1863, after his health failed, Villard returned to Washington. There, with Horace White and Adam S. Hill, he organized a news agency. In 1865 Horace White was made managing editor of the Chicago *Tribune*, and Villard undertook the job of Eastern correspondent for the paper in 1866.

In the same year Villard married Fanny (Helen Frances) Garrison, daughter of the famous abolitionist William Lloyd Garrison. The bride and groom departed for Europe, and from Paris Villard reported on the World's Fair Exhibition of 1867 for the Chicago *Tribune*. On their return to the United States in May 1868, the Villards made their home in Boston, and probably with the added prestige of the Garrison family, he was elected secretary of the American Social Science Association. Villard began to study corporate finance, a subject that would prove to be useful background for a second, and more lucrative, career.

On a trip to Germany in 1873 to recuperate from an illness, Villard was approached by a group of Frankfurt businessmen who asked him to investigate the status of their holdings in the Oregon & California Railroad. The railroad had failed in the bond panic of that year, and the German investors were desperately looking for an agent to watch out for their interests. He returned to the United States as their representative, reorganized the Oregon & California, and became its president.

The first major test of Villard's ability as a railroad entrepreneur came in 1877, when Jay Gould, who controlled the Union Pacific, tried to take over the Kansas Pacific Railroad, a financially troubled company for which Villard was the receiver and in which his German investors held large blocks of shares. After two years of struggle, the railroads merged under terms of an agreement between Gould and Villard which would net Gould a large amount of stock in return for bowing out of the company. Before news of the merger was officially announced, Gould leaked the information to the press, and the stocks soared in value. When Gould felt that the peak had been reached, he sold his holdings. The stock plummeted, but Gould had netted some $10,000,000 in profits.

In 1876 Villard had obtained the controlling interest in the Oregon Steamship Company, which in 1879 he reorganized into a new and larger company, the Oregon Railway & Navigation Company. It became the core of Villard's financial empire and afforded an opportunity to experiment with new ideas and inventions. Villard had been an early investor in Thomas Edison's schemes for electric lighting. Eager to test their possibilities, he had the steamer *Columbia* fitted out with an electric plant in 1879, making it the first electrically lit seagoing vessel.

In 1880 the Oregon Railway & Navigation Company was threatened by the resumption in building of the rival Northern Pacific Railroad. Villard immediately tried to work out an agreement with the president of Northern Pacific, Frederick Billings (1823–1890), to share the territory. Billings rejected the proposal.

Left with no choice, Villard decided to buy stock in the Northern Pacific and get some voting power on the board of directors. Eight million dollars were needed. Villard wrote to fifty acquaintances asking them to invest in a scheme the details of which he said he would not divulge until after the money had been used. The scheme (known later to Wall Streeters as the Blind Pool) was so successful that Villard's office was plagued by people pleading to invest more. Villard agreed to accept another $12,000,000. This additional money went into the Oregon & Transcontinental Company, which he had organized in 1881 with the goal of linking Portland, Oregon, and the newly settled regions of the Pacific Northwest with St. Paul.

In 1881, at the height of his success with the Blind Pool, Villard felt confident enough to invest $260,000 in a square parcel of land 200 feet long behind the newly completed St. Patrick's Cathedral. Villard's site was comparable in size to William Henry Vanderbilt's full-block frontage on Fifth Avenue between 51st and 52nd streets, but Vanderbilt's house was on the preferred west side of the millionaire's Fifth Avenue, while Villard's land was inelegantly placed between the horsecar route of Madison Avenue and the smoke-belching steam locomotives of the New York & Harlem Railroad roaring up Fourth Avenue, a street whose rechristening as Park Avenue was still in the future. The old commuter line linked Prince Street in what is today's SoHo district with Harlem and, later on, the towns farther north along the Hudson. The steam trains deposited their passengers at the outer edge of the city, at 42nd Street, in the terminal built for Commodore Cornelius Vanderbilt by the engineer Isaac C. Buckhout and John B. Snook from 1869 to 1871. The rest of the journey was made by horsecar, for the city fathers had banned the use of steam locomotives downtown.

When St. Patrick's Cathedral was begun in 1858, Madison and Fourth avenues were no more than abstract lines on paper, laid out in the 1811 gridiron pattern plan for Upper Manhattan Island. The *New York Times* of July 12 of that year described the position of the cathedral as on Fifth Avenue, "to where the line of Madison Avenue will run when that street is laid out at its upper end."[1] On paper, Fourth Avenue ran north on a granite ridge. To build the railroad, a deep cut was blasted in the granite, concealing the tracks and muffling some of the noise and soot. The avenue's name was not changed to Park Avenue until 1888, and then only for the distance between 43rd Street and 96th Street.

When Villard purchased his land, the neighborhood was just shedding its earlier image as a catchall of charitable and educational institutions, an area too far north to house fashionable Manhattanites. The New York Institute for the Instruction of the Deaf and Dumb had been on Madison Avenue one block south of Villard's property since 1829, but in 1858 Columbia College had purchased the property and moved north from Park Place. In the 1870s the college surrounded the earlier buildings with new campus additions designed in an asymmetrical Victorian collegiate Gothic style by an alumnus, the architect Charles Coolidge Haight (1841–1917).

Between Madison and Fourth on the next block uptown from Villard's property was the

Catholic Female Orphan Asylum. Across the street between 51st and 52nd streets, to the west of its companion building, was the Catholic Male Orphan Asylum, built about 1867 and designed by the architect of the cathedral, James Renwick (1818–1895). Also in the neighborhood at that time were St. Luke's Hospital on Fifth Avenue between 54th and 55th streets, the Women's Hospital of the State of New York on 50th Street between Fourth and Lexington avenues, and the Nursery and Child's Hospital on Lexington at 51st Street. On the corner of Madison Avenue and 52nd Street a 75-by-100-foot lot was graced by a $50,000 stable built by John B. Snook for William Henry Vanderbilt.

Across Fourth Avenue to the east were rough commercial districts that tolerated the presence of a slaughterhouse, the sheds of the New York and Harlem lines, the F. & M. Schaefer Brewery (between 50th and 51st streets), and the Steinway piano factory one block north between 52nd and 53rd streets.

None of these enterprises, however unattractive, could have brought so peculiar a distinction to the neighborhood as that introduced by its most infamous resident, Mme. Restell (Mrs. Ann Lohman), who in the 1850s built herself a brownstone on the favored west side of Fifth Avenue at 52nd Street. Her connections to society were close—she was a fashionable abortionist. Just after her arrest by the vice squad and her subsequent suicide in 1878, the German-language version of *Puck*, the humor magazine, ran a cartoon showing Mme. Restell's block jammed with pregnant women wheeling carriages laden with infants.[2]

Villard's parcel of land was not vacant when he bought it. The parish Church of St. John the Evangelist had stood on the site since 1859. Its original wood frame structure was built to serve the Catholic population of the then upper reaches of the city until St. Patrick's Cathedral was completed. In 1871 the church burned. The pastor, Father James J. McMahon, rebuilt rapidly, and within a year a new brick church with nave, north and south aisles, and a short transept stood on the site. The sparsely detailed Gothic-style building, which sat 1,200 worshipers, cost $70,000. The cathedral was already well under way in 1871, but the church building was slated to be converted into a school for boys once the cathedral was completed. This planned use perhaps accounts for the lack of ornament on the church. However, the building was abandoned when the parish was suppressed on May 25, 1879, the year the cathedral was finished.[3] The unusual orientation of the St. John's building did not make an economical use of its site, for it was placed with its liturgical east end to the north, and the short transept which faced Madison Avenue would have prevented full use of the land on that side for another structure.

The trustees of St. Patrick's sold the land and the building to Henry Villard on April 16, 1881. On the same day that Villard purchased the 200-foot frontage on Madison Avenue to a depth of 175 feet, a Colonel J. Augustus Page bought the adjoining strip of land running through from 50th to 51st streets and from 175 feet east of Madison Avenue to the 200-foot line. For some reason Colonel Page wanted the church building itself. On July 12, 1881, he sold the lot to Villard for $50,000.[4] On a page of the McKim, Mead & White account book for January 15, 1882, which was used as a blotter, we see in reverse image a letter penned to Colonel Page by the architects as agents for Villard granting him the structure for "the consideration of $250."

Villard seems to have paid less than was offered by another bidder on the lot who planned to build what was described as an opera house (more likely a music hall). The trustees, alarmed by the prospect of such an establishment near the cathedral, accepted Villard's bid, with the restriction that only first-class private dwellings could be erected on the land.

Oswald Garrison Villard, son of Henry and editor of the family-owned magazine, *The Nation*, mentioned in an interview in the New York *Sun* on February 25, 1946, that after his father had bought the land, he offered it to Columbia College at this purchase price so that a chapel could be

View from Frank Leslie's Illustrated Newspaper, *February 15, 1873, of the 126th Street station of the New York & Harlem Railroad. When Henry Villard built his house, the trains still ran in an open cut along what is now Park Avenue. Below: From 1829 to 1858, the "Deaf and Dumb Asylum" occupied the block south of Villard's site. An 1849 engraving after a drawing by E. P. Belden. (Museum of the City of New York.)*

NEW-YORK PAST PRESENT & FUTURE PAGE 94

DEAF AND DUMB ASYLUM.

Hamilton Hall of Columbia College, designed by Charles Coolidge Haight, built 1879 on Madison Avenue between 49th and 50th streets. (Avery Library.) Below: Bird's-eye view of the neighborhood from Harper's Weekly, *November 3, 1894. In the foreground is Columbia College, with St. Patrick's Cathedral at left. (Columbiana Collection, Columbia University.)*

Catholic Female Orphan Asylum, since demolished, in 1890. To the right are the William and Harris C. Fahnestock residences in the north wing of the Villard complex. Left: Cartoon from the German-language edition of Puck *showing Fifth Avenue lined with mothers and infants after the death of Mme. Restell. (Museum of the City of New York.)*

The Church of St. John the Evangelist which stood on the site of the Villard houses from 1872 to 1879. (Avery Library.) Right: View of the east end of St. Patrick's Cathedral from the Villard houses before the Lady Chapel was built. James Renwick's original square English east end, removed to make room for the chapel, now forms the body of the Church of Our Lady of Lourdes, 467 West 142nd Street. (Courtesy of Mrs. Leighton Lobdell.)

built there. Columbia has no record of the offer. If it was made, it apparently was not given serious consideration. In December 1881 the college was indeed looking for land north of the campus for a chapel[5] but settled on a site on Fourth Avenue at 50th Street. In view of the deed restriction, it seems likely that Henry Villard did intend to build a house when he bought the site even if he temporarily entertained other ideas.

Although Villard's property was in the shadow of the cathedral, it was not as close to the building as it is today. Where the 1906 Lady Chapel of Charles Thompson Mathews (1863–1934) now stands at the back of the cathedral there was then only a grass-covered plot. Renwick intended to complete the east end of his church with a magnificent Lady Chapel topped by a 400-foot spire, but economic and technical considerations forced him to cut off the building with a square English east end. Despite this truncated conclusion, Renwick had always hoped to rebuild the east end.[6] The square plot of grass between the east wall and Madison Avenue was bordered on the north and south side by Renwick's archbishop's residence at 452 Madison Avenue and the rectory at 460 Madison Avenue. Both were just being completed when Villard purchased his land.

Within months of his purchase, Villard announced his intention to build several houses that would be entered through a garden rather than immediately from the street. Villard rejected the monotonous uniformity of the private houses of fashionable New York with their repetitive façades fronting directly on the street. His object in building around a garden or court was to emulate the aesthetic arrangement of houses on the outskirts of large European cities and, more practically, to "secure privacy and get rid of tramps, and to live in a quiet and secluded way."[7] The problem of tramps and squatters in the rough world of late-nineteenth-century New York was genuine enough. Within months of the suppression of the Church of St. John the Evangelist, squatters had built shacks all over the land. Oswald Garrison Villard, who toured the property when his father bought it, remembered seeing them there.[8]

Villard's original concept, never carried out, was to landscape both the courtyard and the area behind the houses back to the 200-foot line from Madison Avenue. The houses, then, would be entirely surrounded by gardens. "In the center of the block," according to Villard in an interview for *The Real Estate Record and Guide* of 1881, "is to be a fine fountain, one of the ornaments of the city."[9] Villard's own house was to be on one corner with another house in a separate wing on the other corner, neither of them to be entered directly from the avenue. The interview concludes with a plea that Villard's scheme be followed in the newly settled districts of the city, such as the Upper West Side. In contrast with the prevalent mode, in which one speculative builder after another created separate groups of homes, also one after another, with no overall planning, the editor argued that each block be treated as one parcel and laid out in accordance with the best canons of landscape gardening. Needless to say, this advice went unheeded.

Villard's remarks in this interview seem to confirm that the idea for the general layout of the houses around a landscaped open court came from him rather than his architects and that although it was never put into any stage of preparation, the ground behind the complex, to the 200-foot line back from Madison Avenue, would be a common garden. New York town house rows often had the rear portion of their lots planted with some form of greenery, but these were narrow separate spaces, not communal gardens.

In choosing a garden-enclosed house, Villard, who never lost his accent or abandoned his European style of dress, was capitalizing on his foreignness and employing his own cultivated taste rather than simply accepting the fashions displayed in the mansions of his American-born contemporaries. He may have been partially inspired by the Palace of the princes of Thurn and Taxis in Frankfurt, a city with which he was familiar. Until its destruction in World War II, it was the finest palace in Frankfurt.

Like the Villard houses, the eighteenth-century Thurn and Taxis was built around three sides of a court. Moreover, a large gate with metal fencing closes off the court from the street. Although the style of the Frankfurt palace is French, after a Louis XV *hôtel particulier*, not that of an Italian Renaissance city palace, the general layout and even the roofline of the palace and its wings are similar to Villard's project. The Thurn and Taxis, as is typical of German palaces, is entered off the central axis; this would partly explain why Villard was content to have his own entrance to the right of the courtyard.[10] The back of the main block of the Palace of Thurn and Taxis faces a landscaped French garden. Villard had space for a garden behind his houses, too, but he never got much further than planting grass and some ivy.

Transverse section through the forecourt of the Palace of the Princes of Thurn and Taxis. (Avery Library.)

Top: *Thorwood, the Villard home in Dobbs Ferry, New York, ca. 1867. (Avery Library.)* Above: *Thorwood about 1900, after alteration and enlargement by McKim, Mead & White. The central section of the older house is at left, behind a new columned porch. The house was taken down about 1929. (Houghton Library, Harvard University.)* Right: *Entrance hall at Thorwood, from a drawing in* The Century Magazine, *May 1886. (Butler Library.)*

II

The Genesis of a Design

hen Villard decided to build, he did not have far to look for someone to work with him on the design of his new houses. His wife's brother, Wendell P. Garrison, was married to Lucy McKim, sister of the architect Charles Follen McKim (1847–1909). Shortly before the Madison Avenue property was purchased, Fanny Garrison Villard had hired McKim to carry out renovations at their new house in Dobbs Ferry. Thorwood, a mid-nineteenth-century villa on the Hudson built by the Cochran family, was bought by Mrs. Villard c. 1879 for $28,500. The house stood high on a hill overlooking the river and was one of two similar villas built before 1860 for Thomas and Samuel Cochran by J. E. Burke. The other house, Dunedin, was retained by the Cochran family until the 1890s.

In addition to the alterations on the house, Fanny Villard asked McKim to build a stable. He complied, charging a nominal fee of 2½ percent of the $4,000 commission.

Henry Villard had known the McKim family for a long time. James Miller McKim, a Presbyterian minister and Charles's father, had come under the influence of William Lloyd Garrison and his antislavery writings. (When John Brown was hanged in Charlestown, West Virginia, in 1859, it was Miller McKim and his wife who accompanied Mrs. Brown on her journey to receive John Brown's body, and Miller McKim went with the widow to the burial place at North Elba, New York.) During the Civil War the elder McKim traveled to Port Royal, South Carolina, where in 1862 and 1863 he organized a system of education for the freed slaves. Henry Villard was then a reporter covering the proceedings.

Charles McKim had followed his brother-in-law, Wendell Garrison, at Harvard College. He also spent a great many of his free hours in the Garrison home, Rockledge, in Roxbury, where Henry Villard must also have been frequently present. Although McKim distinguished himself as an athlete at Harvard, particularly in baseball, he was displeased with his engineering education at the Lawrence Scientific School there and longed to go to the Ecole des Beaux-Arts in Paris. Reluctantly, and after seeking the advice of Henry Villard, who was then in Europe on his honeymoon, Miller McKim agreed to his son's wishes.

In 1867, on an allowance of $700 a year, Charles McKim sailed for Paris. Once there, he quickly fell in with two other young Americans studying architecture, Robert S. Peabody

(1845–1917) and Sidney V. Stratton (1845–1921). The outbreak of the Franco-Prussian War in 1870 sent them back to America, and McKim entered the office of Gambrill & Richardson in New York. Of the two partners in that firm, H. H. (Henry Hobson) Richardson (1838–1886), was by far the more important figure. He had studied at the Ecole des Beaux-Arts and was one of the few Americans to have done so before McKim and his group arrived in Paris. (Another early student there was Richard Morris Hunt.) At the time McKim joined the firm, Richardson had found little work in New York. The commissions he did receive seemed to come from Bostonians, many of them people he had known when he was a student at Harvard. He received his first important commission, for Trinity Church, Boston, in 1872. Its design was to give him national and, indeed, worldwide fame. McKim worked on the drawings for Trinity Church and became acquainted with the circle of artists Richardson had commissioned to do the interior of the church: John La Farge (1835–1910), Augustus Saint-Gaudens (1848–1907), and Francis Lathrop (1849–1909), all of whom McKim would later employ on Mr. Villard's house.

Shortly thereafter McKim began to receive small commissions through his family and people he had known at Harvard. When Richardson moved to Brookline, Massachusetts, in 1874, McKim remained in New York, and Stanford White took McKim's place in Richardson's office.

Setting out on his own, McKim took two small rooms at 57 Broadway, where the architect Russell Sturgis (1836–1909) already had his office. Sturgis, for whom McKim had worked briefly before going to the Ecole in Paris, had also employed young Vermont-born William Rutherford Mead (1846–1928). In Sturgis's office, Mead trained as an architect under George Fletcher Babb (1836–1915). After leaving Sturgis, Mead went to Florence to study its architecture and live with his brother, the renowned sculptor Larkin Goldsmith Mead. His stay in Florence over, he returned to 57 Broadway, looking for work. Finding Sturgis out of town, Mead dropped in on McKim, who decided he had enough work to support an associate.

By 1878, William B. Bigelow, who was a fine draftsman, a fellow student in Paris, and McKim's brother-in-law as well, joined McKim and Mead at 57 Broadway, and the three set up practice as McKim, Mead & Bigelow. By 1879, this partnership had changed. Bigelow's sister had left McKim, and he left the firm and was replaced in the office by Stanford White (1853–1906).

In 1880, McKim, Mead & White were hired to do a country house for another future resident of the Villard house complex. Harris C. Fahnestock hired the firm in June to make additions to his seaside house in Elberon, New Jersey, next to that of former President Ulysses S. Grant, and Fanny Garrison Villard brought the firm to Dobbs Ferry in February.

Although the commission in Dobbs Ferry for Mrs. Villard had started modestly, by the end of 1880 her husband seems to have taken an interest in the house. The bills in the McKim, Mead & White account book now change to his name and increase in amount over the next two years. By January 1882 the bills for interior renovation had increased to almost $28,000 and show the involvement of the master woodworker Joseph Cabus and of John La Farge's glass company and various other artisans. Thorwood seems to have become the family's true home—the place to which they would repair in Villard's darkest hour—and over the years additions were made until the house became several times its original size. Mrs. Villard lived in the house until her death in 1928. It was then demolished. Local residents still refer to the place where the house stood as Villard Hill.[11]

William Rutherford Mead, the quiet figure in McKim, Mead & White, provided the stability for the office, a steadying influence which allowed the two very different personalities of his partners to fly off on divergent courses. Saint-Gaudens, a friend of all three, reportedly once drew a sketch showing Stanford White and McKim as balloons going in different directions while being held in the center by Mead standing on the ground.

The firm was to become by the 1890s the most influential in American architecture. The scope of its achievements is partially recorded in a monograph produced between 1915 and 1920 by the Architectural Book Publishing Company as a series of plates of photographs and specially made drawings of their designs.

Stanford White was the only native New Yorker among the partners. He was born into the cultured and moneyed world of Washington Square, the son of Richard Grant White, a music critic, columnist, and Shakespeare scholar, who was also one of the founders in 1865, with Miller McKim and Henry Villard, of the magazine *The Nation*, which Villard would purchase in 1881. The elder White's career did not provide him with as much income as others in his circle, and Stanford grew up with a taste for the good life, but without an income to support it.

The red-haired young White found it hard to concentrate on schoolwork but showed an early talent for drawing and painting. Concerned about his son's future, Richard Grant White consulted John La Farge. The artist discouraged the idea of a painting career, pointing out that White probably would not find it rewarding until quite late in life. Afraid that his son would not be able to support himself as a painter, the elder White decided to place him in an architect's office to study for a more practical career.

Sometime before October 1872 Stanford White was placed as a draftsman in H. H. Richardson's office at 57 Broadway. Richardson had just won the competition for Trinity Church in Boston. The commission justified employing another hand to help with the task. In the spring of 1874, Richardson moved his home and office to Brookline, Massachusetts. There his Harvard College classmates provided him with more commissions than he had received in New York. The move to Boston made White's life more complicated; he now had to shuttle between the two cities.

Stanford White's evident talent for decorative detail and residential design led Richardson gradually to allow him to share in the design of some houses. While working in Richardson's office, White came under the spell of Richard Norman Shaw (1831–1912), whose projects in the "Olde English" style (later erroneously called Queen Anne) filled the pages of British architectural periodicals. Shaw's tile-hung (tile-clad) houses of the home counties of England married well with the wooden shingle tradition of the American Northeast. There has been debate over the authorship of some of the shingle-covered houses designed by Richardson's firm during White's years there. The Watts Sherman house in Newport, commissioned in September 1874, more closely resembles White's work of the 1880s than Richardson's domestic style. Mrs. Watts Sherman said that Richardson suggested that the interiors be decorated by Stanford White. It is certain that White provided the designs for the decoration of the green and gold library, the white and gold drawing room (the actual decoration was done by the French firm of Allard under White's supervision), and the dining room, all of which were actually not completed until 1881.[12] Ten years later, Allard was to redecorate the reception rooms.

White showed enough ability in architectural composition at this early stage in his career to be consulted concerning the tower of Trinity Church. There is a story that John La Farge sent Richardson a group of photographs, including one of the Cathedral of Salamanca, which Richardson felt might contain the seed of a solution for the design of the lantern, and that he in turn gave the photo to White, who made a drawing modifying the Spanish tower to fit the Boston church.[13]

In 1878 White left Richardson's office to go to Europe for the first time. He remained there for a year and on his return in 1879 went to New York, not Boston. There his predecessor in Richardson's office, Charles F. McKim, had by now begun his own firm with Mead. White was offered William Bigelow's place in the firm because, as McKim commented, "White had not had much training in architecture, but he can draw like a house a-fire."[14]

William Rutherford Mead,
Charles Follen McKim, and
Stanford White about 1905.
(Avery Library.)

According to legend, Stanford White began a design for the Villard houses but departed for a trip to New Mexico before undertaking his work. At the same time McKim apparently had become too occupied with the firm's other commissions, many of them buildings for Villard's railroad company, to devote time to the Villard houses.[15]

When Villard assumed control of the Northern Pacific Railroad, McKim, Mead & White were commissioned to build stations, a company hospital, and a hotel for the line's Portland, Oregon, terminus. McKim traveled to Portland in the spring of 1882 to prepare the designs. He designed the hotel, Portland House, around a central court, and construction began that same year. The firm had built only the basement and ground floor before Villard lost control of the railroad. The commission was given to Whidden & Lewis,[16] who completed the since-demolished hotel in 1888. The hotel's arrangement around a central court suggests the client's idea for his New York house. A bird's-eye view of the Portland Terminal Station, published in April 1882, shows that the architects also designed this building around a central court. Although the design for the terminal is different from that of the house in New York and is based, seemingly, on the Cloth Hall at Ypres in Belgium (a favorite design source used by British architects of the Victorian era such as Sir George Gilbert Scott and the firm of Deane & Woodward), the court looks like the one ideally envisioned by Villard for his New York houses. The grass-covered court of the terminal, although much larger than would have been possible in the New York plot, is highlighted in the design by a large fountain. Because McKim was so busy, Mead is supposed to have assigned the execution of the elevations for the house to Joseph Morrill Wells (1853–1890).

Wells is one of the lesser-known figures in nineteenth-century architecture. He was born in Boston and learned his profession in the office of Clarence Luce (1852–1924), who was primarily known for his shingle-style houses.[17] By the mid-1870s Wells had found employment in the Boston office of the architects Peabody and Stearns. He also did some work for Richard Morris Hunt. Hunt, whose work for the Vanderbilts later established his fame, designed a house on Beacon Street in Boston for Martin Brimmer, a friend of McKim who was active in artistic circles in Boston. A drawing of the Brimmer house which appeared in the *American Architect and Building News* in 1877 was drawn by Wells.

While in Boston, Wells met C. Howard Walker (1856–1937)[18] who then worked for John Sturgis of Sturgis & Brigham. Walker noted that Wells was lonely and shy but managed to establish a relationship with him based on mutual dissatisfaction with the then-fashionable English late-Victorian architecture of Colonel R. W. Edis (1839–1927), William Burges (1827–1881), and J. K. Colling (1816–1905). Walker seems not to have known what he wanted to design, but Wells had definite ideas. One night in 1876 Wells dropped into Walker's room with two large rolls under his arm which he unwrapped for Walker to see. Wells had brought large-scale elevations of the Palazzo Cancelleria and the Palazzo Farnese. Walker relates: "They were light in tone, fine in line. I had never seen anything like them. I asked 'did you make these, Joe?' 'Yes, that is architecture,' replied Wells."[19] Wells, who had not been to a school of architecture, nor had traveled abroad, could have based his drawings only on sources such as the plates in the first two volumes of P.-M. Letarouilly's *Edifices de Rome moderne,* which had been published in Paris between 1840 and 1848. One can imagine Wells poring over these volumes. It is obvious that the two buildings that would inspire Wells's work for Villard were one of his active interests six years before he got a chance to employ them in his designs. Wells greatly admired the Italian Renaissance architect Donato Bramante (1444–1514),[20] whom he and his contemporaries believed to have designed the Cancelleria. The date of construction of the Cancelleria, which was built between 1489 and 1496 in Rome, seems to preclude the possibility of any design by Bramante, for he did not arrive in Rome until it was being finished. The question of who did design the Cancelleria still puzzles scholars.

When Walker went to Europe for a three-year stay, Wells was left without a companion in Boston. It may have contributed to his decision to try his luck in New York. Wells appeared at the offices of McKim and Mead in 1879—Bigelow had just departed—and was hired. He must have come with a high recommendation from Peabody, who had been to the Ecole des Beaux-Arts in Paris with McKim. Wells became the first assistant in the McKim, Mead office.

In New York, Wells became part of a circle of artists, sculptors, and architects who were friends of Stanford White. At last Wells had friends of like interests, something he had missed in Boston. Here he "blossomed into an amiable cynic . . . rubbing his hands with mischievous glee when he impaled a sham. He was fond of mordant epigrams, but underneath like Whistler, he had one of the kindest of hearts. . . ."[21] The group consisted of some forty men who gathered every Sunday afternoon for chamber music concerts conducted by Theodore Thomas in the large studio of Augustus Saint-Gaudens at 148 West 36th Street. The inspiration for the concerts had emerged in the course of many evenings Saint-Gaudens, Wells, and the painter Francis Lathrop spent together in a saloon on Broadway at Washington Place. The three had discovered in one another a passion for music and an affection for an elderly bald-headed violinist who entertained there each night in the company of two talentless musicians and an incompetent magician. They engaged the violinist to come play in Saint-Gaudens's studio on a Sunday afternoon, but this simple occasion soon blossomed into something more ambitious.

At Wells's behest, the Standard Quartet was engaged, and a club was organized to split the musicians' $25 fee. By the fall of 1882 the club included Wells, Lathrop, Saint-Gaudens and his sculptor brother, Louis, the painter Robert Blum, Stanford White, Charles McKim, George Fletcher Babb, Thomas W. Dewing (who painted Wells's portrait in 1884), the poet and editor Richard Watson Gilder, and a few millionaires. With a haze of tobacco smoke hanging heavy in the air and a keg of beer delivered weekly, the atmosphere discouraged women from attending, although the actress Ellen Terry once sat and listened until the clouds of smoke drove her away.[22] Wells selected many of the programs and seemed to have finally found his place among the friendly circle. Villard loved Beethoven, and this musical connection may have provided a bond with Wells, although Villard was not a member of the club.

At McKim, Mead & White Wells was held in high esteem, admired for his high architectural standards and appreciated for his sharp wit. Cass Gilbert (1859–1934), who worked in the office, told how Stanford White once burst into Wells's room with one of his drawings in hand while Wells was eating breakfast. "There," he exclaimed, "look at that! In its way, it's as good as the Parthenon."

"Yes," said Wells, "and so too, in its way, is a boiled egg."[23]

In a daybook, Wells recorded his iconoclastic comments on various subjects, noting on music, "We have plenty of patent exterminators for rats, fleas, bed bugs and other vermin; but none for amateur pianists," and on architecture, "In architecture, individuality of style is at best a doubtful merit, and in a great majority of cases a positive (if not fatal) defect or weakness . . ." and "The classical ideal suggests clearness, simplicity, grandeur, order and philosophical calm—consequently it delights my soul. The medieval ideal suggests superstition, ignorance, vulgarity, restlessness, cruelty and religion—all of which fill my soul with horror and loathing."[24]

Wells's views clearly forecast a break in taste. He rejected the Gothic Revival-Picturesque, a prevalent style of the time, in favor of a sense of order. But until July 1880, when he finally was able to travel to Europe, Wells's preferences were based solely upon books. Unfortunately the letters Wells wrote to White from Italy while he was south of Florence have been lost,[25] so we are unable to know what he felt on seeing at last the Roman palaces he so admired. In any event the trip seems to have confirmed Wells's enthusiasm for Roman Renaissance forms. When he returned from Europe, he accompanied McKim to early meetings with Villard at which the initial design studies were developed. In one of these meetings Wells produced a design on the order of what was eventually built, one which seemed more sympathetic to Villard's idea of a European town house and courtyard than White's concept. Villard's childhood home in Zweibrücken was in modified Renaissance style.[26] Wells was put in charge of the design. During the development of the design studies for the house, Villard and Wells became close friends.[27] They seem to have disagreed only on the material for the exteriors of the houses, Wells suggesting light limestone, Villard insisting that traditional New York brownstone be used.[28]

After having been the dominant building material in New York for about forty years, brownstone was going out of style. Wells's suggestion represented not only a change in taste but a matter of practicality. The dark Belleville, New Jersey, brownstone showed poor resistance to New York weather. The late-nineteenth-century art and architecture critic Mariana Griswold van Rensselaer wrote in February 1886, "We once admired our brownstone very heartily; . . . but it is nevertheless one of the most unfortunate substances that ever went by the honorable name of stone—cold and unattractive in color, and too poor in substance to receive carving well. . . ."[29] For Villard's purposes, however, the brownstone was adequate because his design did not depend on carved ornament. It was also considerably cheaper than the white limestone then coming into vogue.

The success of the design of the Villard houses so enhanced the reputation of McKim, Mead & White that it led directly to the commission for the Boston Library. Samuel A. B. Abbott, a trustee of the library who particularly admired the Villard houses, obtained the commission for them. Abbott had followed McKim's career from his Harvard days and persuaded the committee to give McKim's firm the commission in 1887.[30]

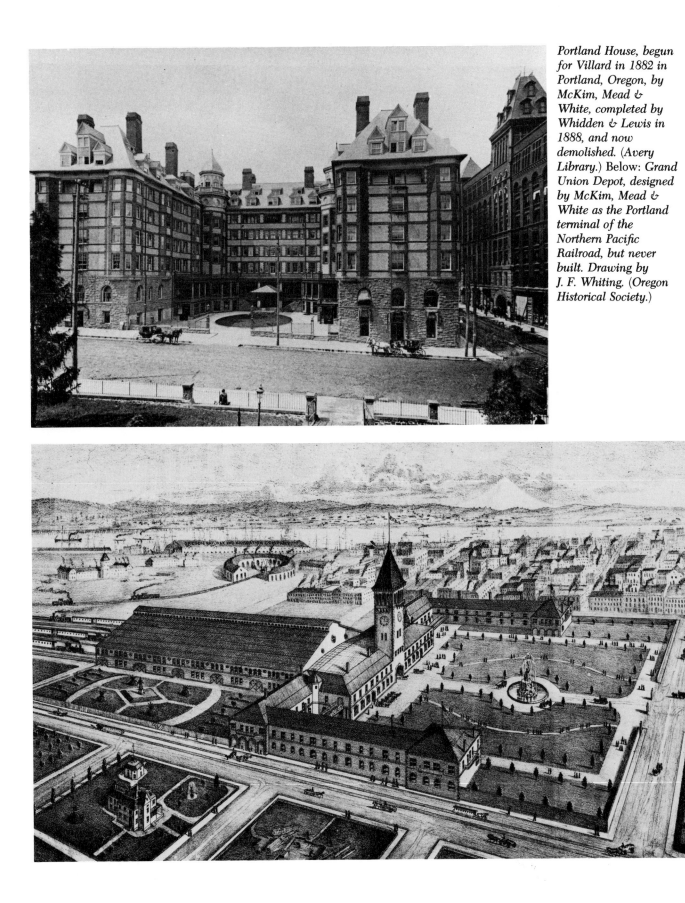

Portland House, begun for Villard in 1882 in Portland, Oregon, by McKim, Mead & White, completed by Whidden & Lewis in 1888, and now demolished. (Avery Library.) Below: Grand Union Depot, designed by McKim, Mead & White as the Portland terminal of the Northern Pacific Railroad, but never built. Drawing by J. F. Whiting. (Oregon Historical Society.)

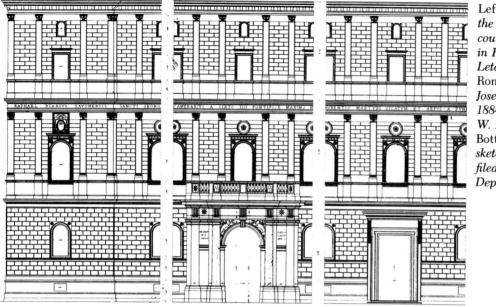

Left and below: *Drawings of the façade and interior courtyard of the Cancelleria in Rome, from P.-M. Letarouilly's* Edifices de Rome moderne. *Bottom, left: Joseph Morrill Wells in an 1884 oil sketch by Thomas W. Dewing. (Avery Library.) Bottom, right: Tracing of a sketch of the Villard houses filed with the New York City Department of Buildings.*

Gathering in Augustus Saint-Gaudens's West 36th Street studio, probably at the time of the memorial concert for Wells, March 6, 1892. Among those present are Saint-Gaudens, Stanford White, Kenyon Cox, Richard Watson Gilder, Brander Matthews, Julian Alden Weir, Francis Millet, Philip Martiny, and probably John La Farge. Dewing's oil sketch of Wells is on the mantel. (Photograph and identifications courtesy R. J. Linder.)

Wells continued working in the office of McKim, Mead & White, his projects ranging from the details of the wainscoting and paneling of the staircase for the Fahnestock house in 1886, to the Russell and Erwin Building in New Britain, Connecticut, the Boston Public Library, the Century Association in New York, and the base for the William Lloyd Garrison statue in Boston.[31]

On December 7, 1889, McKim wrote to White, "Wells is mended again. Your call and his dinner, and the opportunity to lay for Babb, which he never once during the meal failed to take advantage of—all combined to restore him to an amusing vein of good humor, and he volunteered the remark . . . that the upsetting incident of the evening should not be taken too much 'au serieux.' "[32] Wells, who shared the firm's close relationship with George Fletcher Babb of Babb, Cook & Willard, liked to do verbal battle with "Badger Babb." The incident McKim refers to appears to have involved a disagreement over status, for the letter goes on to say:

For my part I would hail his [Wells's] accession as a partner with delight. In spite of his failings, I feel more every day the obligations of the office to him. To my mind he stands alone in the profession for thoughtfulness and a scholarly ability; and I feel sure that you value the soundness of his judgement in composition quite as much as I do. When you think of it, he is wretchedly poor and badly provided for, without a home or any of the good things of this world.[33]

McKim then makes his bid for a partnership for Wells:

He must indeed, as you said tonight, feel the dependent position he occupies at his time of life. It seems to me that it would be only a fair requital of his invaluable service to the office . . . and of the esteem in which we all hold him, to place his name in some manner upon our paper . . . and I do not see that its addition need complicate our affairs, or the case be different from that of Evarts, Choate and Beaman. . . .[34]

(The prominent law firm of Evarts, Choate and Beaman had kept the same name from 1884 to 1894 despite the addition of several new partners, including Prescott Hall Butler, who was McKim's old friend and Stanford White's brother-in-law. McKim was proposing to add Wells to his own partnership, but without changing the firm's name.)[35]

The offer was presented to Wells in January 1890, but he turned it down, saying that he could not afford to "sign his name to so much damned bad work."[36] This sounds like something he would say, but in truth he was dying. He would not live more than three weeks from the time he was offered the partnership. A poignant letter from George Babb, written to Stanford White in 1889 just before the death of Wells, says:

> I understand that Wells is very sick, and the young man I sent to your office says there is fear that he will not live. This destroys all my happiness and peace.... If I could give one ray of pleasure to him by seeing him, please let me know. But if it is true he is beyond hope and that I could not add to his personal happiness, please spare me. I don't know when I would ever get over the shock of seeing him suffer.[37]

C. Howard Walker relates that he came to look for Wells on a cold morning at the office. He was told that Wells had been ill with pneumonia but would be in that day. Wells appeared, looking "very frail," and insisted on taking his friends to see his projects: first to the Century Association, then to the large dining room of the Plaza, which was "reeking with wet plaster." Wells was "enthusiastic beyond his strength," frightening Walker. The next day Wells died.[38] Saint-Gaudens wrote in 1892, two years after Wells's death, "next Sunday, March 6th, come to my studio at 3 P.M. The fellows who formed, during its early days, the quartet will be here to listen to three pieces of music of which Wells was fond. March first was his birthday, and a cherished desire on my part to recall him to our memories every year, in a way he would best like, I will carry into execution for the first time. None but the artists who used to come to the first concerts will be here."[39]

Wells's importance in the firm was for a long time largely forgotten partly because his name never appeared in the list of partners. Still later, in 1928, William M. Kendall (1856–1941), who had entered the office in time to work with Wells on the Villard commission and became a partner in 1906, promoted the idea that Wells did only details of buildings—"the buildings themselves were invariably put together by a member of the firm."[40] This may stem from Kendall's desire to promote his own importance as the first partner added to the firm's roster. But Wells did design the Villard houses. In one of his epigrams he offers the following advice: "To all great men who wish their littleness to remain hidden, my advice is: Never sit for a bust or a portrait, or build a house."[41]

Scheme for the Boston Public Library published in American Architect and Building News, *1888, not exactly as executed by McKim, Mead & White. (Avery Library.) Below: Early photograph of the Century Association building, 7 West 43rd Street, designed primarily by Stanford White and Joseph M. Wells and erected 1889–1891. (Museum of the City of New York.)*

The Tiffany house on Madison Avenue at 72nd Street. Built 1882–1884 by McKim, Mead & White. Based on a design sketched by Louis Comfort Tiffany, it has since been demolished. (Byron Collection, Museum of the City of New York.)

III

Precedents and Parallels

 n April 1882, the same month that the Villard commission appears in the McKim, Mead & White account books, the pages show another domestic commission, a house for the jeweler Charles L. Tiffany at the northwest corner of Madison and 72nd Street. Tiffany wanted a large house which would be divided into three apartments on five different floors to house himself, his daughter and her family, and, at the top, his son, the artist Louis Comfort Tiffany, with his family. Charles Tiffany left the details of the house to be decided by his son in conjunction with the architects, and a drawing by Louis does seem to have formed the basis for White's design.[42]

The Tiffany house parallels the Villard houses to the extent that it was to hold three families within a unified exterior. The differences, however, far outweigh the similarities. The Tiffany families were closely related, while those who were to live in the Villard complex were only business acquaintances. The Tiffany house was actually an unusual private apartment building with a series of interlocking multistory flats, while the Villard complex was to be a cluster of row houses.

In design, the Tiffany house was still Richardsonian. Stanford White designed a monumental house with a heavy base of roughly cut North River bluestone. Despite its name, bluestone is really a brownstone of a light mustard shade.[43] The upper walls of the house were faced Roman brick and topped by a steeply pitched tile roof. The Tiffany house, with its massive walls and Syrian arch of the entry, remains faithful to White's mentor, Richardson. However, its lighter color signals a changing mood in White's evolving aesthetic.

Stanford White collaborated with Louis Comfort Tiffany during the winter of 1881–1882 and produced the design for the house before he departed for New Mexico with his brother early in the spring of 1882. He also conferred with Villard, McKim, and Wells to discuss the design for the Villard houses. White reportedly drew a sketch for a design similar to the one produced for the Tiffany house but had not completed the design when he went away. However, the basic plan for the houses was probably drawn up at those early meetings.[44]

The Tiffany house is an interesting contemporary parallel to McKim, Mead & White's work on the Villard houses. However, it is important to look back at the architectural currents which united in the design for the Villard houses and ushered in the wave of academic classicism typified by the designs for the buildings of the 1893 World's Columbian Exposition in Chicago. A break in the tradition of the uniform brownstone row house had already been inaugurated by Mary Mason Jones's Marble Row and the A. T. Stewart house, and there had been a continuing evolution in the use of Renaissance-inspired architectural detail in New York. When Henry Villard asked his architects to depart from the uniformity of the typical high-stooped, speculator-built brownstone row house, he was following directly in the wake of a triple-headed attack already begun by the heirs of Commodore Cornelius Vanderbilt (1794–1877).

Commodore Vanderbilt was America's richest citizen, but despite his wealth—some $90,000,000 at his death—he lived in modest and slightly worn simplicity in an ordinary row house at 10 Washington Place. The attainment of architectural splendors was a task left to his descendants. The Commodore's eldest son, William Henry Vanderbilt (1821–1885), had moved from the family farm on Staten Island to a mansion at Fifth Avenue and 40th Street in 1867. Although it was designed by John B. Snook, it was a row house and quite ordinary—perhaps a bit fancier than his father's house, but far from palatial.

When the ailing Commodore died, he left the bulk of his great fortune to his son. There were also legacies for William Henry's two eldest sons, Cornelius Vanderbilt II (1843–1899) and William Kissam Vanderbilt I (1849–1920). To the grandson who bore his name, Vanderbilt left $5,500,000 and the modest portraits of the family that hung at 10 Washington Place. To his second grandson, William Kissam, he left $2,000,000. The female children of the Commodore had all but been eliminated from the estate, as had their brother, Cornelius Jeremiah (1823–1882). Although he was not surprised by the will, Cornelius Jeremiah and his sisters contested it; they settled out of court in April 1879.

With the battle over, William Henry's eldest son, Cornelius II, decided to spend some of his money and build a new house. He purchased land at 1 West 57th Street, a plot which had a stable on it belonging to William A. Bigelow and designed by John B. Snook in 1871 and 1872. On August 15, 1879, Cornelius II and his architect, George Browne Post (1837–1913), filed an application with the New York City Buildings Department to erect a $750,000 house with a hip roof and stone cornice.[45]

Post's design for Vanderbilt broke with New York tradition. It departed from the character of the block (there was a typical Renaissance-detailed high-stooped house directly north of Cornelius Vanderbilt's site) in favor of a house in brick and white stone that welded the late Gothic with the early Renaissance, mingling details of both styles in the manner of French châteaux. The house was completed in December 1882.

Just four days after the filing of the application (August 19, 1879) William Henry Vanderbilt filed with the Buildings Department to build a $700,000 house designed by "John B. Snook and J. B. [sic] Atwood." This was actually Charles B. Atwood, who, for this commission, was ghost architect for the famous decorators and cabinetmakers, the Herter Brothers.

William Henry Vanderbilt's new mansion was to be between 51st and 52nd streets. He had purchased the land on the avenue and the contiguous plots to the west of it for $700,000. He asked Snook and the Herter Brothers to work in rapid order, for William Henry felt his time on earth was drawing to a close. He asked his architects to build a triple residence in a U shape with a central entrance off an atrium in the middle of the block. William Henry and his family were to live in one wing on the south side of the complex, and two separate houses were to be created out of the uptown wing for his married daughters.

The houses, like the Tiffany complex, were to shelter three families, but in relatively separate quarters rather than apartments. The entrance to the wings was to be through a central court, as in the Villard houses, but the Vanderbilt entrance was only narrow pavement, not a landscaped courtyard.

The architects had created a boxy house with lavish sculptural detail in a *Néo-Grec* style for William H. Vanderbilt, but as the foundations were being finished, he refused to continue with the building material they had proposed. The Herters, Atwood, and Snook had arranged to use red and black marble sculptural details decorating a face of Ohio freestone. Vanderbilt insisted they use the conventional Belleville brownstone,[46] which was far easier to obtain and quicker to build with than the suggested materials. Thus W. H. Vanderbilt had his house finished in a record two and a half years, moving in on January 31, 1882. Two of the three Vanderbilts, then, had broken out of the New York row house tradition. A third was about to do the same.

William Kissam Vanderbilt had married the incomparable Alva Smith of Mobile, Alabama, in 1875. Socially ambitious, Alva Smith Vanderbilt soon won acceptance in New York and, before her divorce and remarriage to Oliver Perry Hazard Belmont, came close to eclipsing Mrs. Caroline Schermerhorn Astor as the reigning monarch of society.

Just a year after her marriage, Alva Vanderbilt commissioned Richard Morris Hunt to build Idlehour, a country house, at Oakdale on Long Island. Only months after Cornelius and William H. Vanderbilt filed permits with the Buildings Department in December 1879, William Kissam Vanderbilt and Hunt filed a plan to build a four-story house on the west side of Fifth Avenue at 52nd Street at a cost of $200,000. Although it was originally intended to be the most modest of the three Vanderbilt houses, the concept was enlarged. The house, finished in December 1882, probably cost five times the figure filed with the Buildings Department. The architect had tried to persuade the W. K. Vanderbilts to buy the whole block, as W.H. had done to the south, and to allow Hunt to build his François I white Indiana limestone château in mid-block.[47] This was not done, but Hunt managed to rival the lavish cost of W. H. Vanderbilt's house, and in the same way—by specifying and contracting out large amounts of carved ornament for the exterior of the building. William Henry Vanderbilt reportedly paid to have some sixty Italian craftsmen brought to New York to carve the late-Gothic and Reniassance detail on his brownstone houses. The extravagant expenditure (for the sculptors were paid "as artists, not craftsmen"[48]) was known to Charles McKim, who, soothed by their image of stability, used to walk and gaze up at the houses when unable to sleep at night. McKim was mistaken about their seeming immortality; they were to be demolished forty-three years after their completion.[49]

Hunt engaged the sculptors Ellin & Kitson to carve the elaborate ornamentation on the W. K. Vanderbilt house. They also carved Hunt's likeness on the highest pinnacle of the building. Later they worked on the Villard house interiors.

Thus the Vanderbilts came into New York society with a splash. Their highly visible image of success may have appealed to Villard when he contemplated building his own house, but the Roman Renaissance style he embraced expressed a vast difference in taste. Actually the revival of the Roman town palace had experienced a fashionable mode in public and commercial buildings starting in the 1830s, when Sir Charles Barry (1795–1860), architect of the Houses of Parliament, designed club houses along Pall Mall in Roman Renaissance style. In the United States the style appeared first in Philadelphia, in John Notman's Atheneum of 1845–1847, a Barry-like building in brownstone. Shortly thereafter it turned up in brownstone in New York, in Richard F. Carman's 1851–1854 India House (originally the Hanover Bank) in Hanover Square. The style was also used, in a more accurate reflection of Italian models, in Trench and Snook's 1846 whitestone A. T. Stewart store at City Hall and the 1855 Union Club building at 21st Street and Fifth Avenue, designed by Griffith Thomas (1820–1879) and since demolished. Just two blocks to the north of the Union Club, a quasi-Renaissance-style hotel opened its doors—the Fifth Avenue Hotel. Built between 1856 and

Fifth Avenue at the corner of 51st Street in 1894. At left and center are the twin mansions designed by J. B. Snook and Charles B. Atwood for William Henry Vanderbilt and his daughters. At the right, across 52nd Street, is the turreted château of William Kissam Vanderbilt. (Photograph by J. S. Johnston courtesy Museum of the City of New York.)

Top: *The William Kissam Vanderbilt house, designed and built by Richard Morris Hunt.* Above: *The Cornelius Vanderbilt II house, 1 West 57th Street, before its 1893–1894 enlargement by G. B. Post. All these Vanderbilt mansions, completed by 1882, have since disappeared from the New York scene. (Museum of the City of New York.)*

Top: *Griffith Thomas's 1855 Union Club, now gone.*
(The New-York Historical Society.) Above: *The*
Glenham Hotel, completed 1861, now the Albert
Building. (M.G.B.) Right: *Fifth Avenue looking north*
from in front of the Glenham Hotel about 1885.
Beyond the carriage at left is the Fifth Avenue Hotel
of 1856–1857.

1857, this luxurious hotel, designed by Griffith Thomas and the ubiquitous John B. Snook,[50] had the second passenger elevator in the world to be used in a public building. The first was at the Observation Tower of the New York Crystal Palace of 1853. (The Fifth Avenue Hotel and the Haughwout store at 488 Broadway were rivals for the honor of the first commercial use of Mr. Otis's device. The Haughwout store, built for a china and glass importer, is still standing.)

Renaissance revival details were now filtering down to speculative builders, who used them with a total lack of comprehension of the actual proportions of Renaissance buildings, applying them to what Henry-Russell Hitchcock has called "Barry High Renaissance palaces in brownstone."[51]

A fascinating building close to Villard's earlier home at 100 East 17th Steet, and a much more obvious prototype, is the former Glenham Hotel of 155–157 Fifth Avenue at 22nd Street. Now scarcely recognizable, hidden in the shadow of the Flatiron Building, the six-story half-block building covers, in an irregular manner, the northern portion of the block between 21st and 22nd streets from Fifth Avenue to Broadway. The building was completed in 1861. In 1870 it became the Glenham Hotel, with the J & C Johnson dry goods store in the Broadway ground-floor front. The area around Madison Square was becoming the city's fashionable hotel district, but by 1889 the building was being converted into lofts for light manufacturing.

In the realm of large, freestanding private houses for the rich, the dominant mode in the 1870s had become one or more variations on French late-medieval and Renaissance styles, primarily through the influence of the three Vanderbilt houses on Fifth Avenue. The William Henry Vanderbilt house at 51st Street, however, presents a distinctive, chastened, although still eclectic, version of this French mode. Rectilinear Renaissance massing and articulation in terms of columns and pilasters are subtly blended with broad bands of rich bas-relief sculpture, which ranges from a medieval Reims-inspired continuous-leaf pattern at the lowest story to a full Renaissance rinceau at the third.

It was in this climate of French-influenced mansions which were mélanges of Renaissance and Gothic details that the Villard design emerged. Although the Glenham Hotel had brought far more sophisticated Renaissance detailing to New York than the speculator-built brownstones of the mid-century, it is the Villard houses that first exhibited on the brash streets of New York the learned scholarship of Letarouilly and the exquisite proportions of the Roman High Renaissance. Joseph M. Wells, with McKim, Mead & White, succeeded in re-creating features of the Cancelleria and the Farnese Palace in archaeologically correct form and proportions. In their consistent historicism, the Villard houses put to rest the complex eclecticism of the American Romantic tradition. Furthermore, the choice of style had a twofold benefit that would certainly not be lost on Villard the businessman: the economy resulting from sparse ornamentation and the use of brownstone.

The Cancelleria in Rome, Wells's major design source for details, does not present an open courtyard to the street. It is arranged around a central court that is cut off from the street by a long flat façade, and the five-arched portico can be enjoyed only if one goes through the house to the atrium. Villard's open courtyard allows us to see the arcaded portico of the central portion of the houses from the street. The portico is based on the ground-floor arches of the Cancelleria, even to the circular medallion placed on the spandrels between the arches, but the resemblance ends there, for above the portico, on the second and third stories, paired windows replace the loggia of the Cancelleria. Paired windows are not used at all in the Roman building, so this is a substantial break from the model. The departure was brought about by the division of the central portion of the Villard complex into two row houses.

The Villard houses differ from the Cancelleria in other ways. The main entrance door to the Roman palace is asymmetrically placed in the long block and is of a design not used in any way in the New York house. The Villard design adds projecting balconies on the second story of the north and south wings. Most revealing of all is the use of the quoins on the second, third, and fourth stories of the central portion to indicate the points of separation of the central house unit from the side houses. The Farnese Palace, the other Roman palace Wells had drawn from Letarouilly, may have served as the model for the use of quoins and for the elimination of pilasters, features which Antonio da Sangallo (1455–1534) had banished from his palace design.

A third Roman Renaissance palace may also have been a source of inspiration. The garden façade of Baldassare Peruzzi's Villa Farnesina of 1509–1511 is rather similar to Villard's arrangement around a court. Peruzzi's design presents short projections on either side of the house. The central section of the garden façade also has a parti of five round-headed arches on the ground floor. Although the Farnesina is smaller than the Villard houses, the garden façade seems a likely parallel.

The square plot of grass between the archbishop's residence and the rectory of St. Patrick's Cathedral as it was before the addition of the Lady Chapel in 1906 is repeated almost exactly in size and shape by the court bounded by the north and south wings of the Villard houses. The wings of the Villard complex almost align with the two church buildings, and together the two plots of ground originally provided an open space almost as large as Gramercy Park's square green enclosure. Physically, and certainly visually, the impression of a great expanse of greenery was achieved by this perhaps not-so-coincidental alignment of the two groups of buildings.

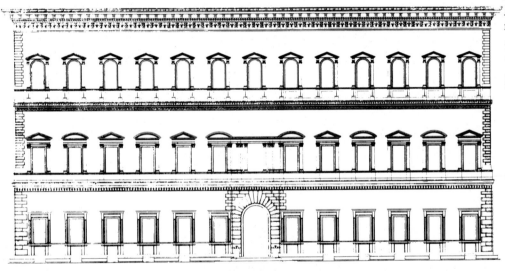

Illustrations from Edifices de Rome moderne *by P.-M. Letarouilly.* Above: *Principal elevation of the Farnese Palace.* Below: *Garden front of the Villa Farnesina.* (*Avery Library.*)

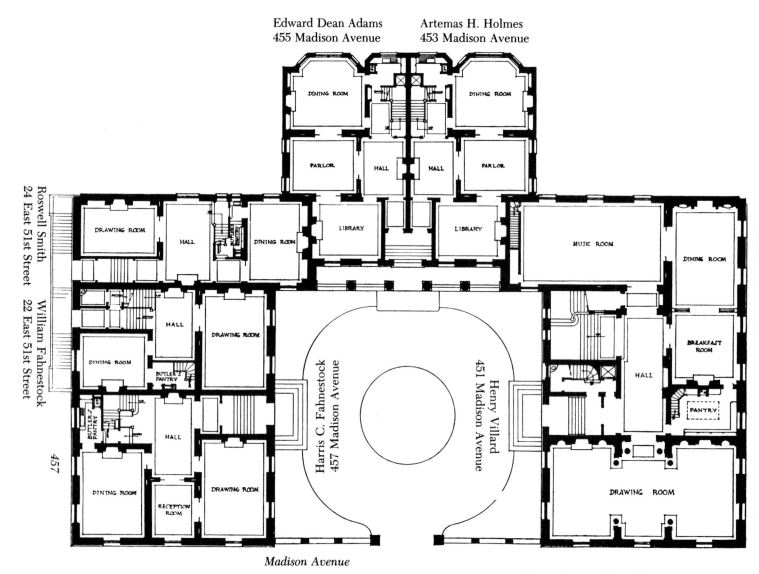

Edward Dean Adams
455 Madison Avenue

Artemas H. Holmes
453 Madison Avenue

DINING ROOM

DINING ROOM

PARLOR

HALL

HALL

PARLOR

Roswell Smith
24 East 51st Street

William Fahnestock
22 East 51st Street

DRAWING ROOM

HALL

DINING ROOM

LIBRARY

LIBRARY

MUSIC ROOM

DINING ROOM

HALL

DINING ROOM

BUTLER'S
PANTRY

DRAWING ROOM

BREAKFAST
ROOM

HALL

457

BUTLER'S
PANTRY

HALL

Harris C. Fahnestock
457 Madison Avenue

Henry Villard
451 Madison Avenue

PANTRY

DINING ROOM

RECEPTION
ROOM

DRAWING ROOM

DRAWING ROOM

Madison Avenue

*Idealized plan of the Villard complex
published in the 1915 monograph of the
works of McKim, Mead & White. This was
the architects' original conception, revived
for the monograph. In the actual execution
of the houses, minor changes were made to
suit the individual owners. In this
illustration, names and addresses of the first
occupants have been superimposed. (Avery
Library.)*

IV

Façades and Finances

ctual construction at the Madison Avenue site began on May 4, 1882, with Villard's own house on the south side of the complex. This was to be 451 Madison Avenue, and it would run some 60 feet north along the avenue from 50th Street, with an entrance within the courtyard, and would extend back 100 feet eastward along 50th Street.

Villard's original plan was to build and sell the five other houses in the complex. A letter of April 2, 1883, from Artemas H. Holmes (1849–1917)[52] makes it clear that foundations were being laid for the two center houses, 453 and 455 Madison Avenue. These were to be approached through vestibules off one large vaulted entry behind the portico. These mirror-image houses were evidently promised to Holmes and to Thomas Fletcher Oakes. Both were associates from the Kansas Pacific Railroad. Villard had brought them to the Northern Pacific when he became its president. Oakes was made vice-president of the Oregon Railway & Navigation Company while Holmes became the attorney.

In the spring of 1883 Villard's railroad fortune seemed secure, and he issued substantial orders to his contractors. The first bill for Villard's house appears in the account book of McKim, Mead & White on February 12, 1884, but it is itemized and probably indicates orders placed many months before. The total is $213,679.28.

While the various artisans were executing the decorative and structural details, Villard's railroad operations were becoming more uncertain. Villard had overspent on railroad construction, hoping to recoup by luring German settlers to the sparsely inhabited northwest territories and increase the payload from his transport lines. In this, too, he failed, and a public relations extravaganza which had been planned to restore confidence in his management of the Northern Pacific actually brought about his downfall.

In August 1883, to celebrate the linking of the railroad from Kansas to Oregon (the last spike was to be driven on September 3), Villard stocked luxuriously outfitted Pullman cars with lavish

Above: *Crow Indians gathered for their September 1883 meeting with Henry Villard at Grey Cliff, Montana. (Photograph by Haynes of St. Paul courtesy Houghton Library, Harvard University.)* Right: *Caricature of Villard in the New York* World, *February 3, 1884. (New York Public Library.)* Opposite: *Henry Villard (at left) standing on a Northern Pacific Railroad locomotive on its maiden run to Portland, September 1883. (Photograph by F. Jay Haynes.)*

foods and a seemingly unlimited supply of vintage champagnes. He invited 350 noted guests, including President Chester A. Arthur, Ulysses S. Grant, and Carl Schurz, as well as delegates representing major investors in Germany and England. Along the route, various celebrations were to provide amusement. At Bismarck, North Dakota, Sitting Bull was brought forward to make a speech. The Sioux chief denounced the stealing of Indian land to give to the railroads, but his remarks were translated into English by an army officer as a hospitable welcome. As the procession crossed North Dakota and Montana, Villard arranged to have grain and vegetables placed along the track to show how rich the soil was along the right-of-way. At Greycliff, Montana, a barbecue was arranged with 1,500 Crow Indians, who in return were to perform a mock scalp dance for the guests as well as take part in a ceremony formally ceding their hunting lands to the railroads.[53]

Instead of impressing the bondholders, the flamboyant journey across the vast empty land alarmed them. At Portland, they abandoned the entertainment and telegraphed their brokers to sell their stock. To add to Villard's troubles, Frederick Billings, former president of the Northern Pacific, and his friends dumped their holdings, causing a panic. Villard went into the market with his personal fortune, estimated at perhaps $5,000,000, in an attempt to buy up enough stock to avert disaster. His efforts were doomed to failure—too many people were selling. By December 1883 the crisis had forced Villard out of the presidency of the Northern Pacific. He had lost all of his backers' money and most of his own. On December 17, 1883, the day he resigned from the railroad, Villard moved his family into the still-unfinished house on Madison Avenue, saying that he could no longer afford to maintain them in their hotel suite.

A spate of headlines followed. For three weeks Villard remained "shut up in his marble palace, refusing to be interviewed."[54] Billings, doubting that Villard was personally impoverished, went to his home on Madison Avenue. There, despite the "atmosphere of fresh mortar and new varnish,"[55] Villard managed to convince Billings that he was truly bankrupt. The argument in financial circles and in the newspapers focused on whether Villard had indeed acted honorably and truly sacrificed his own money trying to save the investments of his friends and supporters. Villard seemed financially ruined and appeared to owe the Oregon Railway & Navigation Company about $320,000. However, some of his assets, including the *Evening Post*, which he had purchased in 1881, were in his wife's name.[56] The house on Madison Avenue, with the remaining lots, was transferred to trustees, so that the other houses might be completed and sold. This indenture of December 28, 1883, was prepared by Villard's attorney Artemas H. Holmes, who on that day became the first to buy one of the residences in the complex.

Villard became ill once his desperate hours with the railroad began. The constant newspaper stories and public curiosity upset him. Crowds appeared at the Madison Avenue dwelling to harass Villard. Many believed that the entire complex of, by then, three houses was a mansion solely for the use of one man—a scoundrel who had betrayed the interests of his friends. Haunted by the publicity, the family fled the house early in the spring of 1884 for Dobbs Ferry. They would never return to their Madison Avenue residence, and in 1886 it was sold to Mrs. Whitelaw Reid. Villard's dream house had become a symbol of his financial failure.

Upon stepping down as president of the Northern Pacific, Henry Villard was voted a salary of $10,000 a year.

Within two short years he was back on solid footing as the United States representative for the Deutsche Bank, and by 1887, with new capital from German investors and the help of his neighbor Edward Dean Adams (1846–1931), he was back on the board of the Northern Pacific. In 1889 he was once again in control of the majority of stock and chairman of the board of directors. For the railroad's Chicago terminal (Grand Central Station, built in 1888–1890), Villard commissioned not his brother-in-law's firm, but Solon S. Beman (1853–1914), architect of the Pullman Company village outside Chicago. Villard himself, back in New York, had taken an apartment in the Tiffany house on Madison Avenue at 72nd Street.

Villard resumed his interests in the Edison General Electric Company and was its president until 1893, when it was reorganized as the General Electric Company. In that year, during another general railroad panic, the Northern Pacific failed again. Villard retired from business and retreated once more to Dobbs Ferry. There he began to write his memoirs, a two-volume work published after his death which concentrated primarily on his years as a journalist before and after the Civil War and only briefly on his years as a railroad financier.[57]

Villard died in 1900 at Dobbs Ferry and was buried at Sleepy Hollow Cemetery, where he rests under a tomb carved by the renowned Austrian-born sculptor Karl Bitter.

Under the terms of the indenture, the trustees were to see to the completion of the houses and the courtyard. Presumably the construction on the three houses on the north side of the complex (457 Madison and the two fronting on 51st Street) began in the spring of 1883, about the same time as the two center dwellings, but in a letter to W. R. Mead on June 17, 1884, Artemas H. Holmes complained that construction of the courtyard had not begun. He insisted that the work be done immediately to make the property more salable, threatening that if the firm's contractor, John Tucker, did not immediately put in the courtyard he would hire someone else to do the job. Some newspaper accounts of the time refer to a "noisy" fountain in the courtyard, indicating some temporary attempt at completing Villard's original scheme, but needless to say, the idea of a splendid fountain in the middle of a beautifully landscaped courtyard was abandoned.[58]

Holmes, who was the first to buy into the complex (in December 1883), purchased the right half of the central block, 453 Madison Avenue. Holmes was born in Galena, Illinois, in 1849 and was admitted to the bar in New York in 1874. In 1877 he was counsel to the Kansas Pacific Railway Company and brought its complaint against the Union Pacific Railroad before the secretary of the interior and the attorney general of the United States. By May 1880 Holmes was friendly enough with Villard to invite him to his wedding. He married Lillian Stokes, the only daughter of Henry Stokes, president of the Manhattan Life Insurance Company. The wedding notice listed Artemas Holmes as the attorney for the Oregon Railway & Navigation Company, as well as other railroads. In November 1881 Holmes was host at a banquet at the newly completed Union League Club in honor of Villard. William Endicott, Jr., Horace White, and Holmes's law partner, George H. Adams, were on the guest list, along with George M. Pullman, J. P. Morgan, and Carl Schurz.

Once the complex had been put in the hands of trustees and the Villards had moved to Dobbs Ferry, it was left to Holmes to pursue the construction and sale of the houses, but little is known about him following the departure of the Villards.[59] His partner, George H. Adams, who was an assistant district attorney for New York City, died in 1898. *Who's Who in New York State* in 1911 listed Artemas H. Holmes as a partner in the firm of Holmes, Rapallo, and Kennedy, at 66 Broadway, and a director of the Lawyer's Surety Company and the Manhattan Life Insurance Company. He lived with his family at 453 Madison Avenue until 1916 and died in August of the following year at Noroton, Connecticut.

Thomas Fletcher Oakes, who was originally scheduled to buy one of the houses, apparently backed out of the plan after Villard's problems arose. The house intended for him at 455 Madison was bought by Edward Dean Adams in 1883. In order to help facilitate dispersal of the indenture, Adams also purchased the house at 24 East 51st Street and joined Harris C. Fahnestock in buying 22 East 51st Street. The house adjoining his (No. 24) was resold in 1886, and that same year his interest in No. 22 was relinquished to Fahnestock for the use of his son William.

Edward Dean Adams was born in Boston, Massachusetts, the son of Adoniram Judson Adams and Harriet Lincoln Norton Adams, and was a descendant of the family which had given the nation two presidents. In 1878 he became a partner in the banking firm of Winslow, Lanier & Company in New York.

Adams's ties to Villard were through the Northern Pacific Railway. He was president and one of the founders of the Northern Pacific Terminal Company, which built and leased the terminal in Portland to Villard's railway. Following Villard's withdrawal in 1883, Adams reorganized the company and backed it with his own capital. Later in the 1880s Adams was to provide a new seat on the board of directors for Henry Villard. Adams had a reputation as a troubleshooter for ailing companies, an ability acknowledged by J. P. Morgan after Adams had solved the organizational troubles of the Central Railroad of New Jersey in 1887.

Railroads were not Adams's only concern. He also worked tirelessly to make the American Cotton Oil Company solvent in 1891. When he refused to take a fee for his work, the directors commissioned Tiffany & Company to make for him an elaborate gold urn studded with jewels.

In 1893 Adams withdrew from Winslow, Lanier to become the United States representative for the Deutsche Bank (a post Villard had held in 1886) and once more took charge of the reorganization of the again bankrupt Northern Pacific.

Once Adams was in the complex, Harris C. Fahnestock (1835–1914) was persuaded to take over part of it. Fahnestock, like Adams, was a partner at Winslow, Lanier & Company. In January 1886 he bought the north wing of the complex. It contained two houses, 457 Madison Avenue and the adjoining residence at 22 East 51st Street. Fahnestock, who had arranged loans for the federal government during the Civil War, had been caught in the railroad bond panic in 1873, when the brokerage firm he worked for collapsed, largely as a result of its backing of the California & Oregon Railroad, but he went on to the bond department of the First National City Bank in 1877, then to Winslow, Lanier. He was also an early client of McKim, Mead & White; they had made additions to his summer house at Elberon, New Jersey, next door to that of former President Ulysses S. Grant.[60] McKim did about eleven houses in this fashionable seaside community between 1877 and 1881.

Harris C. Fahnestock, with his wife, Margaret McKinley Fahnestock (1835–1898), and their children, occupied the dwelling at 457 Madison, in the front of the north wing. The house adjoining it, at the rear, 22 East 51st Street, was for his son, William Fahnestock (1857–1936), who was also engaged in banking and finance. The younger Fahnestock began his career at the First National City Bank and in 1881 opened his own brokerage firm, Fahnestock and Company, which is still in business. Other houses in the complex and the neighborhood eventually were also occupied by members of the Fahnestock family. Although they are known to history by the name of the originator of the plan who lived here so very briefly, there was a time when the Villard houses perhaps might have been more aptly called the Fahnestock houses. It was Harris C. Fahnestock's investment in the houses, along with that of Artemas Holmes and Edward Dean Adams, that saw the plan through to completion.

On September 1, 1886, the house at the northeast corner of the complex, 24 East 51st Street, was sold to Roswell Smith (1829–1892). Smith was associated with Charles Scribner, Josiah G. Holland, and Richard Watson Gilder in the publication of *Scribner's Monthly*. After 1881 he became the owner of its successor publication, *The Century Illustrated Monthly Magazine*. Smith, like Miller McKim, was interested in the abolitionist cause and the education of former slaves. He was also a benefactor of Berea College and financed the construction of one of its buildings, Abraham Lincoln Hall, a Babb, Cook & Willard design. The architectural firm also designed the De Vinne Press Building at 399 Lafayette Street (1885–1886), where the magazine was printed. The building was commissioned by Smith and De Vinne.

When 451 Madison Avenue was sold to Mrs. Whitelaw Reid in 1886, the Villards still owned undeveloped lots behind the complex. In May 1887 Artemas Holmes, acting for Fanny Garrison Villard, sold the lot behind 451 Madison to Edward Mitchell for $21,000. Mitchell, a journalist with the New York *Sun,* commissioned Charles Coolidge Haight, who had designed the collegiate Gothic Columbia College buildings across the street, to build a four-story house. It was completed in late December 1888 at a cost of $30,000.

Next to the Mitchell property was a 20-by-64.8-foot lot, which Holmes sold to Mary P. Hoadly on July 1, 1887. Mrs. Hoadly was the wife of George Hoadly, a former Ohio governor and resident of Xenia. Hoadly may have known his New York neighbor when Whitelaw Reid was editor of the Xenia *News.* When the house was purchased, Hoadly had just moved to New York, where he soon established a successful legal career as a partner in Hoadly, Lauterbach, and Johnson, specialists in mortgages and real estate purchases. Haight designed for Hoadly a house to complement that of Mitchell. The two houses were demolished in 1978.

Houses for Edward Mitchell and George Hoadly built 1887–1888 on East 50th Street behind the Villard complex by Charles Coolidge Haight and demolished 1978. The photograph was taken before a kitchen extension and then a tower were added to 451 Madison Avenue, filling the open lot at the left of the Mitchell house. (Avery Library.) Left: Architect's drawing of the front elevation of the Mitchell house, 31 East 50th Street. (The New-York Historical Society.)

V
The Villard Interiors

Although its entrance is on the south side of the central courtyard rather than through the more prominent central arcade, Henry Villard's house was planned to be the largest and most magnificent of the six. The interiors were planned as a focus and culmination of the entire architectural composition. While the exterior of the complex is in a relatively correct Roman High Renaissance mode, the interiors represent a freer interpretation of that style, an adaptation that is firmly rooted in many of the American design attitudes and conventions of the late 1870s and 1880s. But by comparison to the eclecticism of the period, the Villard interiors nevertheless seem historically accurate and remarkably consistent.

Furniture which incorporated Renaissance motifs was popular in America in the mid-nineteenth century, but the sources of inspiration were wide, embracing Renaissance details of the sixteenth and seventeenth centuries from all Europe, not just Italy. In general, the taste for Renaissance-derived interior decoration in the America of the 1850s and 1860s seems to have come from France and the ateliers of the Ecole des Beaux-Arts. It is difficult to determine precisely when and in what manner Renaissance motifs first made their appearance in the architectural interiors of the American affluent, but some features, particularly in wood paneling, adorned all three of the New York Vanderbilt houses built and decorated between 1879 and 1881. The Herter Brothers' largest commission, and Christian Herter's last decorative undertaking, was the William H. Vanderbilt house, where 600 to 700 craftsmen were employed for a year and a half on the furniture, carpets, mosaics, and marquetry.[61]

As far as the Villard interiors are concerned, the most influential aspect of Herter's designs for William Henry Vanderbilt were the pilasters inlaid with rosewood, mother-of-pearl, and brass which framed the library doorways.

The Villard house was complete enough by December 1883 to allow Villard and his family to move in. The partially decorated rooms were photographed for the fourth section of *Artistic Houses*, a luxurious limited-edition volume illustrated with pictures of fashionable interiors. In its pages the Villard rooms join those of the illustrious of the age, the Vanderbilts, George F. Baker, and H. Victor Newcomb, among others.

Opposite: *The original entrance doors to Henry Villard's house at 451 Madison Avenue. The doors were modified many years ago. (Avery Library.)*

Considering the intense business and social rivalries of the period, it is not surprising that Villard should have emulated to some extent the decorative trappings of his neighbors, but the Villard interiors seem chaste and sober in comparison. As *Artistic Houses* noted:

> To artists and connoisseurs Mr. Henry Villard's house presents at least two general features of unusual significance. With all its magnitude and costliness . . . it has preserved a chaste simplicity . . . and a profound loyalty to what is delicate and self-repressive. No attempt at ostentation appears . . . but good taste as understood by persons of refinement and education and experience.

Although the effect of three rooms enfilade (as seen through an open vista in a photograph of the Vanderbilt drawing room, great hall, and picture gallery) is similar to that of the Villard drawing room, great hall, and music room, the restraint of the Villard interior is notable. The Villard rooms also have columns flanking the doorway, but the Vanderbilt gilded putti, elaborate surrounds, and heavy portières are absent in Villard's house. In fact, portières are missing in all the pictures of the Villard interiors, a notable exception to the rule of taste in 1882 and 1883. Possibly some were planned but not yet installed when the photographers arrived.

Unlike the Vanderbilt houses, where exotic rooms provide *Belle Epoque* glamour, the Villard house had no Moorish, Japanese, or Chinese rooms. The only unusual room was the so-called medieval guest room. Its medieval elements are hard to discern. Though they are less elaborate in their appointments than the Vanderbilt interiors, the sober and restrained mood of the Villard rooms is no less rich in effect.

Although the Villard interiors are unified in tone, distinctive nuances of detail in each suggest that various artisans were responsible for the decoration of the principal rooms. The triple drawing room facing Madison Avenue, for example, is quite dark by contrast to the partly finished music room, which displays a lighter and more "French" touch. An analysis of the extant bill books helps us understand these differences more clearly. The account books list amounts paid to the craftsmen commissioned by the architects to carry out the work.

Notably missing is any reference to individual *artists'* commissions, such as Saint-Gaudens's well-publicized contributions and the attribution of the mosaics of the principal hall to glassmaker and attorney David Maitland Armstrong (1836–1918). Contemporary accounts refer to work in the house by Augustus Saint-Gaudens and his lesser-known brother, Louis; Augustus Saint-Gaudens himself refers to his "sculpture decoration in Villard House, 1882"[62] in his own list of work. Armstrong is not mentioned in newspaper accounts, but this may be due only to his lesser reputation at the time. Armstrong may have designed the hall tile mosaics, and the work perhaps was executed by Pasquali and Aeschlimann, marble mosaicists of 321 East 28th Street, who were paid $20,000 for mosaic work in the house. Pasquali and Aeschlimann also did marble mosaics for the Vanderbilt and Goelet houses.

Numerous contemporary accounts attribute the authorship of the "Pax" relief in the entrance hall and the relief over the mantel in the dining room to Augustus Saint-Gaudens. However, no bill for these works has been found. As for the marble mantelpieces, they were probably based on European models and executed by either Louis Saint-Gaudens or the sculpture firm of Ellin & Kitson of 519 West 21st Street. Louis Saint-Gaudens's name does not appear in the bill books, but Ellin & Kitson billed the architects $30,081 for their work.

The only artist whose name does appear in the bill books is Francis Lathrop, who painted mythological subjects for the dining-room ceiling panels. For this he was paid just over $2,800. Lathrop's inclusion among the craft accounts might indicate that he was not yet considered a "fine artist." The city directories of the period list him as a "decorator" at 72 West 4th Street.

Left: *Interior of the William Henry Vanderbilt House. Vista from the drawing room through the hall and picture gallery to the conservatory.* Below: *The Villard reception room, hall, and music room en filade, December 1883. (Avery Library.)*

Views of Henry Villard's triple parlor about 1884. (The New-York Historical Society.) Right: Portion on the 50th Street side of the house. The drawing room fireplaces are still in the house but the elaborate wood marquetry over them has been removed. (Avery Library.) Opposite: Detail of the original decoration of the wall in the center section. (The New-York Historical Society.)

The records suggest that the selection and supervision of various decorators and craftsmen were made by McKim, Mead & White with different designers responsible for individual rooms. Stanford White, himself an inspired genius of a decorator, assisted in the main hall and dining room. He and Saint-Gaudens collaborated on the zodiac wall clock on the landing. Someone else in the office, possibly Francis Bacon (1856–1940), designed the woodwork for the principal rooms of the house during the winter of 1882–1883.[63] It is likely that the work itself was executed by Joseph Cabus, who had done the interiors at Villard's house in Dobbs Ferry. Cabus heads the list of decorative firms in the accounts with a bill for $99,000 for woodworking, making it highly probable that he was responsible for much of it. Cabus's work at the New York State Appellate Court on Madison Square Park survives, along with the Villard interiors, as a reminder of the skill of the late-nineteenth-century "fine arts" craftsmen.

The furniture for the house came mainly from Sypher and Company, which presented a bill of almost $26,000, with the Marcotte Company supplying a lesser share at about $10,000. That of the music room, in its lightness, looks like Marcotte's work. Other furniture, perhaps that for the dining room, came from the A. H. Davenport Company of Boston, which maintained a New York branch during this period.

Herts Brothers of 806 Broadway (not to be confused with the more famous Herter Brothers) were probably responsible for one room; the bill was over $10,000. C. R. Yandell and Company, cabinetmakers of 6 East 18th Street, received commissions amounting to $5,000. Yandell was known for "illuminated" leather wall coverings, and this may be what they supplied to the Villard house.

The renowned Cheney Brothers provided silk fabrics. It could not have been a large amount, as the bill was less than $900. Equally modest are the $1,000 or so to La Farge's decorative glass company and Tiffany's glass studio. The Society for Decorative Arts, the needlework organization founded in 1877 by Candace Wheeler (1828–1923) probably provided fine embroideries for the house, as there is a bill from it for $2,772.

Of Villard's personal possessions in the house we know little. A Renaissance Madonna and Child attributed to Antonio Rossellino (1427–c. 1478) was donated to the Metropolitan Museum of Art by Villard in 1899. It may have been intended for the house and then simply removed when the family departed for Dobbs Ferry in 1884.[64]

A notable feature of the architectural interiors of the last quarter of the nineteenth century was the interplay of talent stimulated by the collaboration of painters, sculptors, and architects on a single project. At Trinity Church in Boston, H. H. Richardson's great work of 1872–1877, the first of these major collaborations took place. The talents of Richardson and his office, which then included Stanford White, were combined with those of John La Farge and Augustus Saint-Gaudens to produce the church's splendid interior. The following year a similar collaboration of artists worked on the chancel of St. Thomas Church at Fifth Avenue and 53rd Street. La Farge and Saint-Gaudens provided the building, designed by Richard Michael Upjohn (1828–1903), with decorative schemes for the chancel. These were sadly lost when the church burned and was demolished in 1905.

The first major collaboration of noted artists and architects in a residential commission was the Cornelius Vanderbilt II house of 1879, where the talents of La Farge and Saint-Gaudens combined with those of the architect George B. Post to create one of the finest interiors in America. Saint-Gaudens's contribution was sculpture; John La Farge's was ceiling paintings and stained-glass windows for the house. La Farge had studied stained-glass techniques in England in 1873 but then developed a technique of his own for making opalescent windows that included insertions of thicker chunks of glass which were often jewellike in color and shape. (There has long been debate about who first popularized artistic glass in America—John La Farge or Louis Comfort Tiffany.)

The interiors of the Villard house, then, are solidly within this collaborative tradition—the work of numerous hands brought together in a manner reminiscent of rooms in the William H. Vanderbilt house of 1879–1881, but in a restrained style that is without the effulgent variety of that ensemble. The consistent pursuit of Renaissance style in the Villard exteriors, their avoidance of the prevalent taste for mingling Moorish, Japanese, and other exotic and picturesque design elements signal a change in taste that had a profound influence in the remainder of the nineteenth century.

The scale of Villard's house was magnificent. On the first floor there was a triple parlor, a large hall, a grand music room, and a huge dining room served by a pantry. The basement of the house was used, in the typical fashion of the day, as a service area, containing a kitchen, laundry, wine room, and servants' dining room. Beneath the basement was a cellar which held three large boilers, one with a high-pressure machine for pumping water to the immense storage tank located on the fifth floor. Water pressure was needed not only for the internal plumbing but also for running the hydraulic passenger elevator. The billiard room, usually a prominent feature of upper-class Victorian homes, was banished to the basement. Villard might have been following a precedent set in a McKim, Mead & Bigelow house, that of Frederick F. Thompson at 283 Madison Avenue (1879–1881), where the billiard room and bowling alley also were located in the basement.

From the entrance, one ascended a short marble stair within a mosaic-vaulted grand vestibule that led to a large, groin-vaulted hall.[65] The principal rooms of the Villard house are on what is actually the equivalent of a traditional row house parlor floor above a basement rather than a true Roman *piano nobile*, which was always a full story above the street. The vaults and floor are adorned with mosaic in varied patterns, while the walls are faced with Mexican marble inlaid with Siena marble.[66] This hall is in the style of the period, a "living hall," a room to sit in as well as a circulation area. The fireplace has a marble mantelpiece; above it is a sculpture in bold relief of a woman with a child on either side that is titled "Pax." The sculpture is attributed to Augustus Saint-Gaudens, who also prepared the models for several works in the dining room of the Villard house in 1882.

Left: *Fireplace and overmantel designed for Cornelius Vanderbilt II by Augustus Saint-Gaudens and others. (The Metropolitan Museum of Art. Gift of Mrs. Cornelius Vanderbilt, Sr., 1925.)* Above: *Augustus Saint-Gaudens in his studio. His subject is Mrs. Grover Cleveland. (Avery Library.)*

Right: *Main hall of the Villard house, looking west toward the drawing room doors, about 1883. (Avery Library.)* Below: *View from the drawing room end of the hall, looking toward the music room.* Opposite: *Inner entrance leading from the vestibule to the main hall. The glass panels, designed by either Tiffany or La Farge, are still in place in the fanlight and sidelights. (The New-York Historical Society.)*

Opposite: *Living hall
fireplace and overmantel
designed by Saint-Gaudens
for Henry Villard. Above:
Detail of the overmantel
relief. Left: Door to the left
of the fireplace leading to the
breakfast room. (Museum of
the City of New York.)*

At the eastern end of the house is the large two-story music room—an impressive space which would have made a distinguished setting for Sunday afternoon concerts. The music room was not completed when Villard moved into his house and was not finished until the Whitelaw Reids bought the house and decorated it in their own manner.

An 1883 photograph shows the music room as it looked when Villard moved in. One can see that the upper walls and barrel vault were painted in a light color. Below, wall paneling about ten feet high is decorated with a delicate design of musical instruments and garlands carved in low relief and painted a creamy white.

Saint-Gaudens may have suggested the insertion in the walls of the music room the plaster casts of Luca della Robbia's 1431–1448 marble "Cantoria" from above and on either side of the doorway of the left sacristy of the Cathedral of Florence. He had come to admire fifteenth-century Italian sculpture while studying in Rome in 1874 and had returned to America with casts of works by Della Robbia, Donatello, Ghiberti, and Verrocchio, which he hung on the walls of his studio.[67] On November 1, 1883, an entry in the accounts of Henry Villard with McKim, Mead & White lists $250 paid for a cast of "singing boys," surely the bill for the ten plaster panels, five of which form a horizontal band across the back (north) wall of the music room behind the balcony and five on the south wall opposite it. The plaster panels were assembled in an order different from that of Della Robbia's splendid original. They illustrate Psalm 150, the text of which is inscribed in the Della Robbia piece, but not in Villard's panels. Apertures in the wall are screened by openwork carving which was designed to conceal the pipes of an organ, although it is not known whether one was ever actually installed. An early photograph shows the room furnished with music stand decorated with motifs of the mythological figure Pan and rows of upholstered chairs with straight high backs, armrests, and short legs ranged along the walls. The room was intended to have a movable painted ceiling which could be raised or lowered to meet the acoustical requirements of the program, but this was never installed.[68]

The dining room as it was during the Villard's brief occupancy can be seen in a late 1883 photograph. It was entered from the hall through sliding doors embellished with a decorative pattern of tiny nailheads. The furniture and woodwork were reported to be of richly carved English oak. Running along the bottom of the frieze are inlaid panels with sentimental mottoes in German, English, French, and Latin cut out of white mahogany. Cased beams embellished with decorative moldings span the ceiling. The Lincrusta panels between them have an intricate tracery of stylized leaves and flowers and inset with paintings of mythological figures done by Francis Lathrop. At the east end of the room is the principal fireplace. The entire fireplace wall is said in one report to be of Numidian marble; in another it is described as Siena marble.[69] Three crouching figures representing Joy, Hospitality, and Moderation above the fireplace are by Saint-Gaudens. At the sides are sculpted niches with integral basins and bas-relief dolphins, indoor fountains which "spouted the Croton."[70] The fireplace has since been moved twice, once when the Whitelaw Reids extended the dining room into a new tower addition at the back of the house in 1910–1911, and again when the tower was taken down in 1978. In 1980, it became the focal point of the lobby of the new hotel erected behind the complex.

The dining room then measured about 20 by 60 feet. It could be used as one large room or scaled down by having drawn across it an almost ceiling-high carved oak screen, thus turning the west end of the long space into a more intimate breakfast room. The fireplace at the breakfast room end is of marble, reportedly from Verona, and bears across its front a procession of animals.[71] This mantel, said to be a copy of an old Italian piece, was later duplicated in a pinker tone of marble and installed in the Whitelaw Reid country house, Ophir Hall, when the house at 451 Madison was redecorated by McKim, Mead & White.

The Villard music room. Left: The south wall with five panels copied from Luca della Robbia's Cantoria in the Sacristy in Florence above the door. The man in the chair is not identified; it may be Wells, as this is a very early photograph. (The New-York Historical Society.) Below: Opposite end of the music room in 1883. Five more panels from the Cantoria are above the balcony.

*The Villard dining room. Opposite: Dining room
fireplace with overmantel figures designed by
Saint-Gaudens. (Museum of the City of New York.)
Top: View of the dining room, looking east, with its
original furnishings. (Avery Library.) Above and left:
Details of the ceiling paintings and doors.
(Photographs © Nathaniel Lieberman.)*

Above: *Zodiac clock designed by Augustus Saint-Gaudens and Stanford White for the wall of the first landing of the grand stair of the Villard house.* (The New-York Historical Society.) Right: *Second floor landing of the grand stair showing the original wall and ceiling treatment. Each baluster has a different carved design.* (Avery Library.)

To the left of the breakfast room fireplace, a door led to a serving pantry. After the addition of a tower extension by the Whitelaw Reids in 1910–1911, the door gave access to a new reception room. The dining room, and probably also the rest of the house, were lit by hanging gasoliers and sconces with fluted glass shades.

A $5,000 bill from Edison Electric Lighting Company in February 1884 indicates that electric fittings were included in the original house in anticipation of the extension of residential electric service from a new power station which was to serve the neighborhoods north of those in the original Pearl Street plant.

The Villard house is the first residence known to have been built with Edison electric fittings designed to be compatible with a city-wide power distribution system rather than an independent generator, but not until the Whitelaw Reids took over the house did electrified sconces and picture lights actually replace gas illumination.

The furniture commissioned by Villard for the dining room includes two massive tables and a set of chairs carved in an eclectic nineteenth-century adaptation of the Tudor-Elizabethan style evident in furniture used throughout the principal rooms of the house. Most distinctive of the pieces in the room is a large sideboard with a shell motif in its base. This is similar to pieces illustrated in photographs of several other interiors published in *Artistic Houses* which were from the hand of Francis Bacon, who also designed furniture for H. H. Richardson and Herter Brothers during this period. This room is represented in a three-volume picture book of Francis Bacon's work for the decorative firm of A. H. Davenport, which he joined in 1885.[72]

Three rooms facing Madison Avenue, the reception room and two flanking drawing rooms, are articulated only by screen walls of columns and panels. These spaces could be combined *en suite* for entertaining. The color scheme of the rooms' furnishings, according to one report, intermingled red with cream. The red-stained cherry wood paneling had elaborate marquetry inlays of white mahogany, satinwood, holly, and mother-of-pearl. The wall surfaces of the drawing rooms were hung with terra-cotta silk embroidered in a yellow-orange thread. This fabric was repeated on the furniture upholstery. One description of these silk panels calls them a light yellow color, not terra-cotta, and states that the embroidery is red, not yellow-orange,[73] but concurs that the furniture was covered with the same material purchased from the firm of James Cheney.

The entire suite was fitted with elaborate marquetry in mahogany in an "Italian" Renaissance design. On the pilaster columns surrounding the doors, highlights of the marquetry, picked out with mother-of-pearl, include an intertwined motif enclosing the date of the room—1883—and the initials of Henry Villard and his wife, Fanny. At the sides are four recessed shell-topped wood niches with shelves which were meant to hold bibelots. This room, removed from 451 (as were the other two drawing rooms in 1891 when the Whitelaw Reids redecorated these principal rooms on the main floor), is now part of the paneling in the front parlor and bedrooms of what was the Reid country house, Ophir Hall. The original plaster ceiling decoration, onyx fireplace mantel, and parquet floors were retained in the Madison Avenue drawing room despite the Reids' extensive renovations.

The grand staircase rises in a two-story alcove off the north side of the hall. Large vertical sections of Siena marble heighten the effect of its splendid size. Parcel gilding emphasizes the motifs of the alcove ceiling. At the arcade above, each carved marble baluster is of a different design. On the wall is the famous clock designed for the house by Saint-Gaudens and Stanford White, a square marble panel with signs of the zodiac cut in low relief on colored marble inlays. Gilded rays of cut bronze-doré filigree work form the clock face, while the silvered metal clock hands and pendulum float in front of the surface of yellow marble. Ascending the stair, one passes through a marble-arched arcade into the large central hall on the floor above, a space made more intimate in scale

Left: *Stairway which led from the second floor hall to the third story. The grilled door to an elevator is seen through the arch at the right. This wooden stairway and the elevator were replaced by a fireproof stairway in 1948.* Below: *Third floor living hall during the Villard occupancy.* (*The New-York Historical Society.*)

Right: *A guest room on the second floor was en suite with Henry Villard's library. Below: The library. Motifs in the bookcase doors are publishers' colophons. (The New-York Historical Society.)*

Opposite side of the guest room adjoining the library, photographed in 1883 before the house was fully furnished. (Avery Library.)

and warm in feeling by a dominance of wood and leather in place of the monumental marble and mosaics of the formal "living hall" below.

On the second floor facing Madison Avenue was Villard's library, which was *en suite* with a guest room. Both the guest room and the library had heavy cross-beamed ceilings studded with iron bolts. The walls were hung with deep crimson and gold brocade with gold threads woven into the pattern.[74] The two rooms had an attached dressing room and bath. The library, which is described as being of stained cherry and mahogany,[75] had an elaborately worked wooden fireplace the overmantel of which was a mate to that of the guest room fireplace. Bookcases in the library were decorated with large medallions inlaid with light wood in which the colophons of celebrated printers and publishers of the past are carved. The guest room contained "fine old pieces of furniture"[76] in late-seventeenth-century style, including a canopied bed, a bureau, and the mantel. The oak paneling of the guest room was treated to match the furniture. The room, as shown in an early photograph, appears incomplete. A curious chair in the library, which may be one of Villard's seventeenth-century pieces or may be a contemporary reproduction, has the name John Powers carved across the back and the place-name Peterborough below the seat. This second-story suite was replaced with a large drawing room running the full width of the house by McKim, Mead & White during the 1910–1911 renovation by the Whitelaw Reids. Elements of Villard's library were disassembled and reincorporated in Whitelaw Reid's study in the new tower addition at that time.

A contemporary account of the other bedrooms and guest rooms of the upper floors provides the description that they were of "painted woods, and decorated with extreme simplicity and beauty."[77] Although Mr. Villard's bedroom was by one account on the fourth floor,[78] it was probably on the third with those of the rest of his family. An hydraulic elevator, unusual in a private house of the period, made access easier to those upper floors. Villard's own bedroom, probably never photographed because it was never finished, remains undescribed to us. One photograph of the upper floors as occupied by Villard is of a large bathroom which was probably on the third floor. The photograph substantiates a contemporary report: "There is no attempt at luxurious decoration in these bathrooms, but they are eloquent in marble, porcelain and white enamelled walls of becoming cleanliness."[79]

The family area seems to have been on the "upper floors to which a flight of stairs leads" and was reported to have "Cretonnes [which] have been chosen in design and specially prepared with a view to the character of the house. . . . The ceilings are lower and cherry lends its worth of tint for the dominant coloring."[80] It would seem that for all the grandeur of the principal rooms of the house, the Villard family preferred a warm, cozy space at the top of the house for their own use.

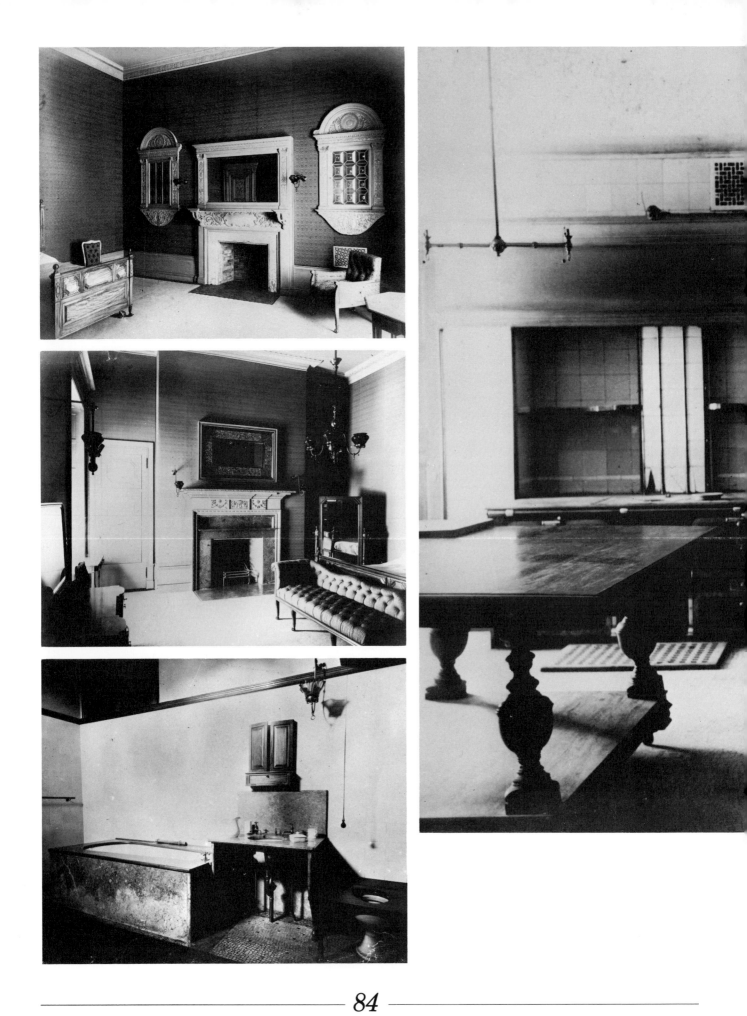

Opposite, top: *One of the bedrooms on
an upper floor.* Center: *Another bedroom.
Gasoliers provided lighting in all the
rooms.* Bottom: *Henry Villard's
bathroom, a model of simplicity for its
time.* Above: *The basement kitchen had
an ambitious hot-water heater.*
(*Courtesy The New-York Historical Society.*)

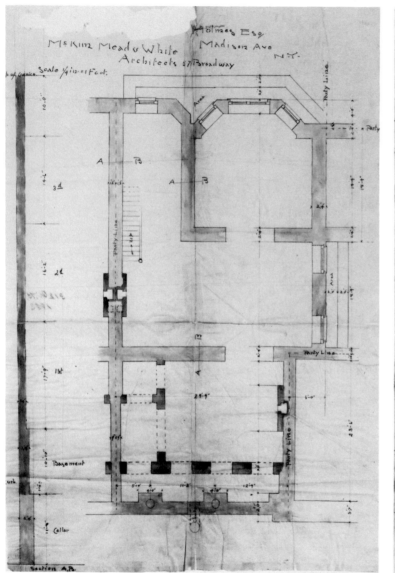

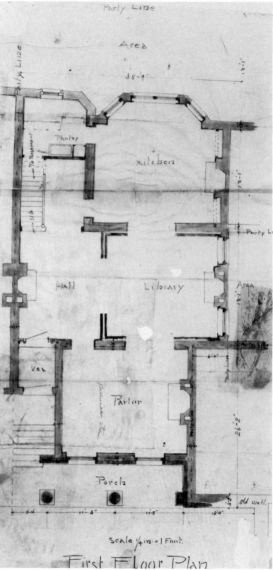

Architects' sketches for the basement and first floor of the Artemas Holmes house, 453 Madison Avenue, filed with the New York City Department of Buildings.

VI

Other Inside Stories

The Artemas H. Holmes House, 453 Madison Avenue

lthough Artemas H. Holmes was a friend of Villard's and slated to live next door to him in the complex, we know from correspondence that he refused the services of McKim, Mead & White's contractor, John Tucker, for the completion of his house and the interior. Instead, he used a contractor named John Banta, to build his portion of the façade from the McKim, Mead & White plans and elevations. Holmes feared that the lavish ideas of Villard's "stylish" architects would make the house too expensive, so he insisted on a modest and conservative interior in the popular Queen Anne mode.

A few bills for interior details of the Holmes house do appear in the McKim, Mead & White account book for the fall of 1884, and three letters survive from their correspondence with Holmes. Dated between 1883 and 1885, they are written on the stationary of Holmes and Adams at 35 Wall Street. In a letter of January 5, 1885, Holmes refuses to pay the architects for the specifications they had given Banta, claiming that Villard should assume the cost because the insistence on uniform façades was his idea.[81]

The only surviving original drawing for the design of the Holmes house is a plan and tracing for the exterior unearthed in a New York City Department of Buildings file. The plan shows only the basement and first floor and the extent to which it basically conforms to the plan published in the McKim, Mead & White monograph.

In 1917 the house was purchased by Mrs. Elisabeth Mills Reid and subsequently leased to Barclay H. Warburton, founder and retired publisher of the Philadelphia *Evening Telegraph*. The house was occupied until the early years of the Depression by his daughter Mary, whose mother was Mary Brown Wanamaker, daughter of John Wanamaker. Warburton continued to hold the lease until 1935.

No photographs have been found of the interiors of the house as they were during the Holmes occupation or the ownership of Mrs. Reid. An elevator was installed in 1920, but there is no record of any other structural changes. Of all the houses, this one suffered the most extensive renovation after World War II. The changes, and the lack of evidence that its interiors were ever particularly distinguished, make it basically the least interesting of the houses.

Opposite: *Entrance to 455 and 453 Madison Avenue. Within the vaulted entry, twin doors led to the vestibules of the Edward Dean Adams house on the left and the Artemas Holmes house on the right. (Courtesy Mrs. John G. Winslow.)* Above: *Edward Dean Adams. (The Metropolitan Museum of Art.)*

The Edward Dean Adams House, 455 Madison Avenue

fter purchasing 455 Madison Avenue, Edward Dean Adams asked McKim, Mead & White to build an extension to the existing shell of the house. This was to house a service area with an additional staircase and a dumbwaiter and, on the upper floors, extra bathrooms and a dressing room. Plans and elevation for this alteration of July 16, 1885, are on file with the New York City Department of Buildings, along with a cost estimate of $2,800 for the job.

Mrs. Leighton Lobdell, the daughter of Edward Dean Adams, grew up in the New York house and at their country home, Rohallion, in Rumson, New Jersey. Her memories of 455 Madison Avenue provide an intimate view of what the house must have been like in the 1890s—a welcome compensation for the lack of photographs from that period.

Mrs. Lobdell remembers the lawn behind the houses where she would let her dog out each morning and where, in summer, the grass cutters could be heard from inside the house. At first there was no central heat in the house, but there were eight fireplaces. The house was lit by gas; electricity was introduced in 1891. A cast of Verrocchio's "Colleoni" stood in the living hall, and George Inness's "Peace and Plenty" hung on the wall along with Winslow Homer paintings her father collected.

Mrs. Lobdell and Lillian Holmes, the young daughter of Artemas Holmes, used a code of shoe taps on the party wall to communicate with each other at night. Mrs. Lobdell remembers her neighbor Harris C. Fahnestock as an elderly man sitting in the library window at 457 Madison Avenue, watching people walk by.

Perhaps most significant is Mrs. Lobdell's impression that her parents regarded Rohallion as their real home and the Madison Avenue house as merely a *pied-à-terre* in the city, a place that before 1883 was meant to be a corporate "perk" provided to its executives at nominal cost by the Northern Pacific.

A photograph taken about 1900 shows Mrs. Adams's boudoir, the center room on the second floor of the house. It was flanked by the study and the master bedroom.

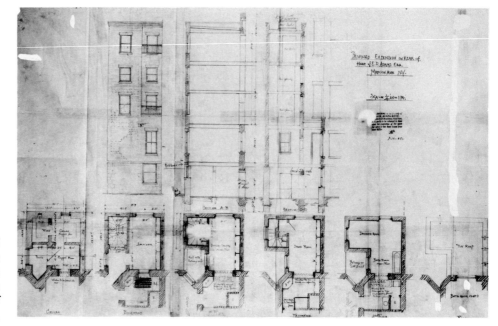

Drawings for the 1885 McKim, Mead & White extension to 455 Madison Avenue filed with the New York City Department of Buildings.

After the death of his wife in 1922 Edward Dean Adams sold the house and moved to Rohallion. This, too, was a McKim, Mead & White design. The house was begun in 1887. ("Rohallion" is a Gaelic term meaning "little red hill." Adams had heard it while on a shooting trip to Scotland. He gave the name to the house in reference to the red color of the earth in Rumson.) Adams sold Rohallion shortly before the 1929 stock market crash; it was too large to maintain. The new owners had it redesigned in the Tudor manner in 1929–1930, and the house is still standing.

After the departure of Edward Dean Adams, his house was purchased by Helen Fahnestock Campbell, who presented it to her daughter, Mrs. Clarence Gaylor Michalis. Photographs taken in 1922 and 1941 show the original entrance hall with the staircase and paneling designed by Francis Bacon for A. H. Davenport in collaboration with McKim, Mead & White. In the frieze surrounding the upper portions of the parlor floor living hall were burnt wood panels executed *in situ* by James Fosdick, and a filigreed clock that is similar in character to one shown on drawings for the Harris Fahnestock interior. The filigreed brass elements are smaller versions of the zodiac clock on the grand stair of the Villard house designed by Saint-Gaudens in collaboration with Stanford White. Above the entrance hall was a shallow leaded-glass oval dome. Similar devices were used in the two Fahnestock houses to bring light to the stair halls. A glass lantern hung from the dome. In a post–World War II renovation, the broad step of the staircase landing and the scrolled newel post were removed, and an elevator doorway was cut at the first landing level. The finish and detail of the living hall remained otherwise untouched. The use of large horizontal sheets of bleached mahogany veneer was unusual for the period.

The parts of the Edward Dean Adams and Artemas Holmes houses that extended eastward from the main body of the complex were demolished in 1978 to make way for The Palace, a new hotel. However, the interior of the Adams stair hall with its beautiful ceiling and paneling was carefully dismantled and preserved and has been presented to the Brooklyn Museum by the developer of the hotel. Paneling from other parts of the house, such as the dining room, has been incorporated into public rooms in the hotel.

The reception room of the first floor had a decorative surface treatment on the frieze above the cornice which appears to be papier-mâché or Lincrusta. The ceiling was molded plaster in low relief. An unusual feature was the wall panel of pierced wood carving alternating with pieces of beveled glass mirror. The portières in the rooms were left by Edward Dean Adams. The details of the shell motif in the recessed wooden niches flanking the drawing room fireplace were similar to the details in the woodwork at the Villard house at 451 Madison Avenue.

Boudoir of Mrs. Edward Dean Adams, ca. 1900. Below: Rohallion, the Adamses' country home in Rumson, New Jersey, with their daughter Ruth (later Mrs. Leighton Lobdell) riding on a pony. (Courtesy Mrs. Leighton Lobdell.)

The stair hall of 455 Madison Avenue in 1941. Right: A light well pierced the floor at the second floor level. Chains suspended from the center of an elliptical glass dome above it supported a glass globe. Below: The oval well and James Fosdick's burnt wood panel designs seen from the first floor. Bottom: Fireplace at the reception level with the pendulum of the filigreed brass clock in motion. Opposite: The stairway. A door in the back wall at the mezzanine level gave access to an elevator. Inset: Mr. and Mrs. Clarence Gaylor Michalis, who succeeded Edward Dean Adams as residents of 455 Madison Avenue, with their daughter Helen Louise, now Mrs. John G. Winslow. (Courtesy Mrs. John G. Winslow.)

Rooms on the principal floor of the Michalis residence at 455 Madison Avenue in the 1920s and 1940s. Right: A corner of the drawing room in 1941. Below: Library, looking toward the reception hall. Bottom: Vista from the library through the dining room in 1922. (Courtesy Mrs. John G. Winslow.)

Two views of the dining room of 455 Madison Avenue in 1922. (Courtesy Mrs. John G. Winslow.)

Kitchen in the basement of the Michalis house. Below: Second floor bedroom, looking east. Opposite: St. Patrick's Cathedral viewed from the portico of the complex, ca. 1922. Charles Mathews's Lady Chapel had replaced Renwick's square east end, but Rockefeller Center had not yet been built. (Courtesy Mrs. John G. Winslow.)

Harris C. and Margaret McKinley Fahnestock.
Opposite: *The north wing ca. 1941. (Courtesy Mrs. John G. Winslow.)*

The Harris C. Fahnestock House, 457 Madison Avenue

lthough the Harris C. Fahnestock house in the front of the north wing is the symmetrical complement to Villard's house in the opposite arm of the complex, it is only one-third as large and was never conceived of as being as elaborate in its interior use of rich materials. It was built as a shell, but drawings of 1886–1887 that still exist in the McKim, Mead & White archive at The New-York Historical Society show the details of the interiors. Initials in the corners of the drawings reveal that they were drawn by various members of the McKim, Mead & White staff. Photographs of this house in its original state show the extent to which the McKim, Mead & White drawings were followed. There are details and motifs that bear a striking resemblance to those in the Villard, Adams, and Roswell Smith interiors. A paneled stair rail and pierced screen enclosure are similar to those at the Smith and Adams houses. The initials on the drawings of the wooden wainscot panels of the stair enclosure are those of Joseph M. Wells. The paneled wainscot was topped by brass nailhead decoration and pressed leather, a treatment often used by Stanford White, George Fletcher Babb, and other designers of interiors in the 1880s. In a modest way the mosaic floor pattern of the hall and entry area and the elaborate window treatment of the library reflect the rich ornamentation of the Villard entrance hall.

The vertical hall with its deeply coffered ceiling is an urban version of the living hall, a mid-nineteenth-century English country house feature which was developed in America by H. H. Richardson. By the 1880s the living hall had become a prominent portion of the American

Above: *Clarence Fahnestock in 1918. (Courtesy Mrs. John G. Winslow.)* Top: *The reception hall of the Harris C. Fahnestock residence in the 1890s. The paneled enclosure at the right of the fireplace conceals an elevator. (Courtesy Clarence F. Michalis.)* Right: *McKim, Mead & White study of the fireplace wall of the reception hall. (The New-York Historical Society.)*

ANNO DOMINI MDCCCLXXXVI

Side

shingle-style houses located in popular East Coast summer resorts, such as Newport, Rhode Island, and Manchester, Massachusetts. The hall became much more than an area of transit. It was a central gathering place where visitors and family members could gather in a corner to converse or relax. It is this dual purpose of the hall that differentiates the living hall from the large central halls occasionally found in American country houses earlier in the nineteenth century—spaces which were really just large vestibules. An important feature of the living hall was the fireplace, and one is found in all the halls of the Villard complex.

The dining room of No. 457 had a built-in sideboard similar to the one designed for the Villard house and visible in the earliest photograph of the Villard dining room. In the parlor were features which seem similar to the redecoration of the Villard house double drawing room and reception suite done by the Whitelaw Reids in 1891. The mantel and mirrored overmantel are identical in character and detailing. The design of the elaborate bas-relief plaster cornice and decorative ceiling is also rather like that done for Whitelaw Reid, and the dining room ceiling vault had a cast plaster medallion design much like the one in the Roswell Smith house.

The library of the Harris C. Fahnestock house (designated as a reception room in the idealized plan on page 54) apparently was changed in the execution to include double doors opening into the dining room. A photograph taken in the 1890s and the architects' drawings for the design of the floor show the additional opening. Drawings also indicate art glass for the arch above the window that is similar in spirit to that in the fanlight above the Villard entry in the south wing. The design of the library dome resembles that of the one decorated with gold leaf which was in the vestibule of the Adams/Michalis house.

Like Villard's house, the Fahnestock house at 457 Madison is entered from within the courtyard. It is the second largest and second most important of the houses. Harris Fahnestock must have contemplated joining it with 22 East 51st Street when he bought it, but he would have been prevented from doing so immediately by a restrictive clause in the deeds probably put there to protect the exclusivity of Villard's portion, which was then up for sale. The unification was not achieved until 1922–1925, after his son William had inherited the house and the restriction had expired.

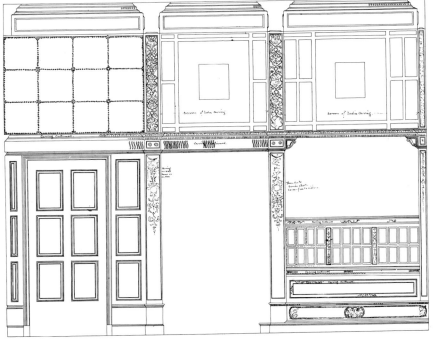

Details of the stair enclosure in the reception hall of the Harris C. Fahnestock residence shown in a McKim, Mead & White study. The stair enclosure and fireplace wall were removed in the 1920s during extensive renovations which combined this house with that of William Fahnestock at 22 East 51st Street. (The New-York Historical Society.)

Dining room of 457 Madison Avenue. Right: Architects' study of the fireplace wall. A door at the left leads to the butler's pantry. (The New-York Historical Society.) Below: A view of the room in the 1890s reveals how closely the McKim, Mead & White designs were followed. (Courtesy Clarence F. Michalis.)

Left and bottom: *Two views of the drawing room ca. 1890–1895. (Courtesy Clarence F. Michalis.)*
Below right: *McKim, Mead & White drawing of the east wall of the drawing room. (The New-York Historical Society.)*

Library of the Harris C. Fahnestock house. Right: View from the drawing room doorway, looking north toward the dining room. (Courtesy Clarence F. Michalis.) Below: Details of the decoration for the arches over the doorways, the window wall, and the domed ceiling. Beveled plate-glass panels were indicated for either side of the window seat. (The New-York Historical Society.)

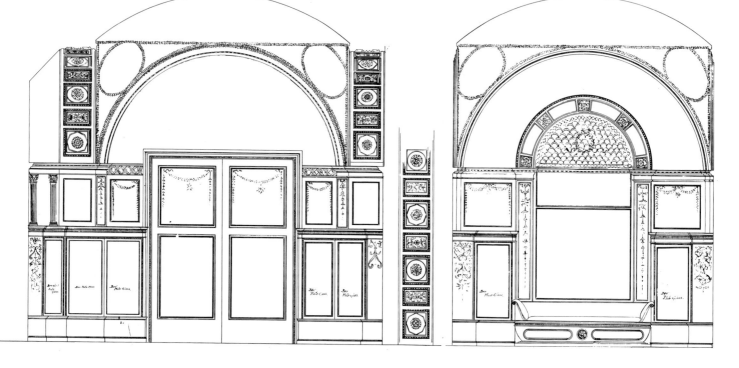

Portraits by Zouloga of Julia and William Fahnestock. (Courtesy Mrs. John G. Winslow.)

The William Fahnestock House, 22 East 51st Street

riginally the house at 22 East 51st Street was in some ways the least impressive in the Villard complex. It was sandwiched between two other houses and, like any typical New York brownstone, had windows only on the front and back. Instead of an entrance through the courtyard, it originally had a high stoop fronting on 51st Street. Edward Dean Adams, who had purchased it jointly with Harris Fahnestock, sold his share to Fahnestock in 1886, and he in turn gave it to his son William, who in 1898 married Julia Strong Goetchius.

The plan of the house closely follows that which appeared in the monograph; this is verified by McKim, Mead & White drawings now in the collection of The New-York Historical Society. The original interiors, done in 1887 and 1888, resembled other houses in the Villard complex in the use of a mezzanine level in the main staircase hall to accommodate a storage pantry. The characteristic living hall with fireplace was retained here, although it is relatively small. The design included an elevator, a feature not initially found in all the houses and, as at Nos. 455 and 457, an oval well over the staircase, although at No. 22 this appears only in the upper floors. Over the ceiling of the reception hall there was a square inset glass skylight that formed part of the floor in the story above.

In 1922 William, who had inherited the house at 457 Madison (his father had died in 1914 and his elder brother, Clarence, in Verdun in 1918), engaged Charles Platt to combine it with his house at No. 22. A previous scheme to combine the two houses exists among the McKim, Mead & White drawings of 1886 but was never executed. The Platt design made far more extensive changes than this proposed scheme. William Fahnestock apparently preferred Platt's fashionable French-inspired style to that of the original architects. In 1911 he had engaged Platt to design his country house in Katonah, New York; he had also had him remodel a house in Newport, Rhode Island.

Charles A. Platt's 1922 proposal for exterior changes to 22 East 51st Street. As executed, a single large window was substituted for the Palladian arrangement two stories above the new doorway. Opposite: Platt's plan for combining the principal floors of the two houses in the front of the north wing, with a single main entrance from the courtyard. Dotted lines represent original stairways, walls, elevator, and chimney masses. (Charles A. Platt Collection, Avery Library.)

Platt's extensive renovations were primarily carried on in the interiors of the houses. The courtyard and Madison Avenue façades show no evidence of the internal rearrangements. Exterior changes are restricted to the 51st Street side, where the original door to the house, which was at the top of a high stoop with a square transom above it, was removed. New window openings similar in character, size, and alignment to the rest of the façade were created. Inside, the rearrangement of the grand stair as shown in the façade study and plans from the Charles Platt archive in the Avery Architectural and Fine Arts Library of Columbia University is a slightly different version from the one that was actually executed. There was a proposal to place windows on each side of the existing opening in order to create a Palladian window at the stair landing. This would have been masked inside by a larger stained-glass panel set in a thin metal frame. Instead, a large asymmetrically placed metal-framed window was set directly in the exterior façade, disturbing the rhythm of the original fenestration pattern.

From the time the houses were combined until his death in 1936, 457 Madison Avenue continued to be William Fahnestock's Manhattan address.

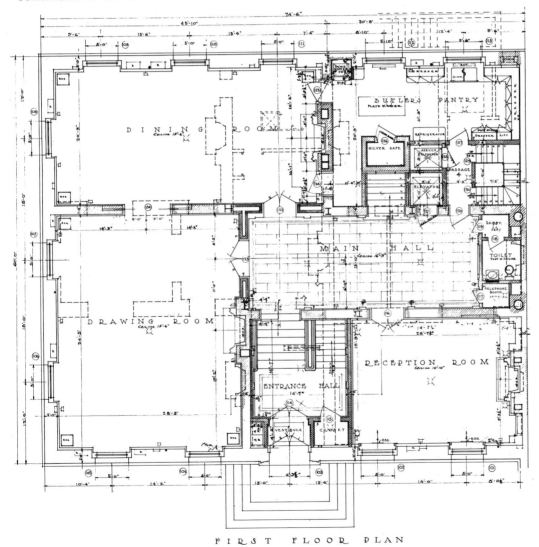

FIRST FLOOR PLAN

The north wing interiors after Platt's 1922 alterations. Pale colors, gold leaf embellishment, and tapestries replace the 1886 McKim, Mead & White dark paneling in most of the rooms of the parlor floor. Opposite page, above, left: *The drawing room. Interior French windows conceal outer double-hung sash. Above, right: The main hall. Bottom: The dining room. Above, this page: Dark paneling was still in favor in the library.* (Photographs by Wurts.) Left: *A magazine illustration shows details of the design for the woodwork and parquet of the reception room.* (All courtesy of William Platt and Geoffrey Platt.)

Roswell Smith. (New York Public Library.)

The Roswell Smith House, 24 East 51st Street

The house at 24 East 51st Street was begun and completed under the terms of the indenture placed on the Villard complex in December 1883. Its first owner, Edward Dean Adams, sold it in September 1886 to its first resident, Roswell Smith. Before moving in, Smith hired the firm of Babb, Cook & Willard to alter the unfinished house. Although the Babb, Cook drawings for the alteration have not been found, the Buildings Department files supply information about the renovation.[82] A small extension was added to the east side of the house, reaching 11 feet into the garden behind the complex. The extension was only on the basement and first story but it was 53 feet 6 inches long. The entrance to the house, which had been from a high stoop on 51st Street, was moved to a portico, which was also built out into the garden area. To link the new entrance, openings were made in the east wall on the first story. The stoop was removed, and the former entrance door was changed to a stained-glass window. The covered porch provided by Babb, Cook & Willard gave the narrow Roswell Smith house a more impressive access route, though one in a *retardataire* style.

The interior of the Smith house was also altered. It had never been finished by McKim, Mead & White. George Fletcher Babb of Babb, Cook & Willard modified the staircase and paneling. By opening new passages in the walls and concealing others with partitions, he also revised the general layout.

In the last years of the 1870s and early 1880s, Babb was highly regarded for his interior work. In fact, he did "the best interior in New York, from an artistic point of view,"[83] for a house being built by McKim, Mead & White for C. T. Barney at 10 East 55th Street, just before they did the Villard wing of the complex. Babb, who had been informally connected to McKim, Mead & White in 1879 and 1880, was probably one of the few architects in New York to whom they would not have objected as a "decorator" for one of their houses, although the alteration and extension are much more Victorian in spirit than the Villard house.

The house changed hands again in 1910, when Harris C. Fahnestock bought it. He later presented it to his daughter, Helen Fahnestock Campbell. In 1928 Helen Campbell was remarried in Paris to John Hubbard, and thereafter she divided her time between Paris and New York. The house became the property of the Archdiocese of New York in 1949, although Mrs. Hubbard retained a life interest and continued to live there until her death in 1955.

Directly behind the Villard complex at 30 East 51st Street there was until recently a house built by McKim, Mead & White in 1886–1888 for Gibson Fahnestock, a son of Harris C. Fahnestock, as a gift from his parents. It was very similar to a since-demolished residence that the same architects had built for Phillips and Lloyd Phoenix in 1882–1884 at 21 East 23rd Street. Both were of brick with Renaissance detail such as bead and reel molding and a heavy cornice. The lot where the Gibson Fahnestock house stood has been incorporated in the site of The Palace.

Above: *Helen Fahnestock Hubbard, who succeeded Roswell Smith as the resident owner of 24 East 51st Street.* Left and bottom: *Views of 455 Madison Avenue and 24 East 51st Street from the northeast showing the porch vestibule, and gallery designed for Roswell Smith at left, and, in the background, a glass-enclosed service entry to the basement of the Adams/Michalis house. (Courtesy Mrs. John G. Winslow.)*

Above: *The Villard houses about 1890. (Museum of the City of New York.)* Left: *Elisabeth Mills Reid and Whitelaw Reid, who succeeded Henry Villard as residents in the south wing shortly after the houses were built. (Butler Library.)*

VII

At Home with the Whitelaw Reids

n November 1886 the Villard house was sold to Elisabeth Mills Reid, wife of the editor and publisher Whitelaw Reid, for $350,000, the sum of the indenture which had been placed on the house.

Reid, like Villard, was active in the antislavery cause and had covered many of the same battles during the Civil War. His stories from the battlefront had earned him recognition as the dean of Civil War correspondents. In his early years as a journalist Reid worked for the Xenia *News*, in Ohio, where he wrote editorials in support of the abolitionist cause and became active in political circles, spending the summer of 1860 as secretary of the Republican County Committee.

In 1868 Horace Greeley offered Reid a staff job on the New York *Tribune*. Reid continued to engage in politics after the war, and in 1872 he managed Horace Greeley's campaign for the presidency. In 1888 he was sent to France as United States minister, and in 1892 he ran for Vice President on Benjamin Harrison's unsuccessful Republican ticket. In 1897 President William McKinley sent Reid to England as representative at Queen Victoria's Diamond Jubilee. The following year Reid served as a member of the commission which arranged the terms of peace that ended the Spanish-American War. In 1905 he was made ambassador to Great Britain, a post he held until his death in 1912.

Whitelaw Reid's paper anticipated Villard's break with architectural fashion in New York. In 1870 Reid had assigned Clarence Cook to write about New York architecture for the *Tribune*, and commented on the "dreary miles of brownstone fronts"[84] that housed the city's wealthy men.

Upon Reid's marriage to Elisabeth Mills in 1882, his father-in-law, Darius Ogden Mills, had purchased the *Tribune*, making Reid the editor. The family tie with the paper was to endure until its demise in the 1960s. The Mills wealth enabled the Reids to acquire both the Villard house and a thousand-acre country estate in Westchester. Ophir Farm had belonged to Ben Holladay, a financier whose manipulation with western railroad stocks had contributed to the debacle of 1873. Holladay had named the farm after a western mine which had yielded him a fortune. The Reids rechristened it Ophir Hall. Following a fire in July 1888 McKim, Mead & White were retained to rebuild and redecorate the house.

The Reids occupied the Villard house late in 1886 or early 1887 and immediately began to complete some of the half-finished rooms to their own taste. An 1887 magazine account reported: "There have been some changes. The luxurious boudoir and medieval guest chamber . . . have been made one with the already spacious library, and a more notable room devoted to the service of the student and man-of-letters is not to be found in the city."[85]

Right: *Entrance hall of 451 Madison Avenue after it became the home of Mr. and Mrs. Whitelaw Reid. (Museum of the City of New York.)* Below: *John La Farge:* Portrait of the Artist, *dated October 26, 1859. (The Metropolitan Museum of Art, Samuel D. Lee Fund, 1934.)* Below, right, and opposite: *Views of the music room taken in 1977 show La Farge's paintings for the lunettes and the elaborate Stanford White ceiling decorations commissioned by the Reids. The upper wall covering and wall sconce globes are of a later era. (Photographs © Cervin Robinson.)*

Above: *Marquetry paneling of the Villard triple drawing room reinstalled in Ophir Hall, the Reids' country home.* Above, right: *Painted panels succeeded the marquetry in the drawing room at 451 Madison Avenue. (Avery Library.)* Right: *A new reception room replaced the parlor floor pantry in Stanford White's 1891 redecoration. An unobtrusive door in the wall at right led to the drawing room. (Museum of the City of New York.)*

When the house was purchased, Reid commissioned paintings from John La Farge at the urging of his friend John Hay, who was the owner of a newly finished house by H. H. Richardson in Washington, D.C. (later known as the Hay-Adams house). At each end of the music room La Farge painted huge lunette pictures representing music and drama. Legend says that the face of Elisabeth Mills Reid is represented in the lunettes, but this is unsubstantiated. La Farge knew Hay well but was not closely acquainted with the Reids. He began the paintings in 1887, working in collaboration with Stanford White, who was about to devise a new decorative scheme for the room. La Farge originally believed that the ceiling barrel vault would be painted blue, but White then changed his mind about the color, opting for the scheme which has caused the music room to be known since by the name of the Gold Room. La Farge thus found himself having to redefine the colors of his paintings. They were completed in 1888. No artificial light source is apparent in the original Villard scheme; electrified wall sconces and a central ceiling light were added by the Reids. It is difficult to decide if the "amber opalescent glass" in the windows of the music room during the Reid occupancy is the glass for which Villard was billed by La Farge. The research of Barbara Helen Weinberg indicates that the glass was his work.[86] It was similar to the grisaille glass La Farge provided for Trinity Church in Boston in 1876, but no positive attribution has been made.

In 1891 (the same year the ornate Tiffany and Company screens and interiors installed in 1882–1883 were removed from the White House), the Whitelaw Reids renovated and redecorated their principal drawing rooms facing on Madison Avenue. McKim, Mead & White, under the direction of Stanford White, removed the elaborate woodworking and inlaid panels, creating one large elaborate drawing room with marble columns and pilasters topped by bronze-doré Corinthian capitals. To achieve this large open space, concealed steel girders were inserted to carry the load once held by masonry bearing walls. New painted panels replaced the old marquetry ones. Although the newer "French" taste was now displayed in the drawing room for the guests of vice presidential candidate Reid,[87] the discarded interiors were not destroyed. The wooden marquetry panels were installed in several rooms of the newly rebuilt Ophir Hall, where they are still to be seen; the building is now the main administrative center of Manhattanville College.

In the New York House, the Villard service pantry behind the drawing rooms was remodeled and turned into a reception room. A "secret door" concealed behind a hinged marble niche provided a discreet escape from dull receptions. Vestiges of the doorway and decorative plaster ceiling of the reception room remain behind the post–World War II renovation of the premises by the Archdiocese of New York.

The dining room of the Villard house was kept much the same as it was under the previous owners, but the Reids' paintings were illuminated by electric lights, and the gasoliers were removed. In September 1896 Whitelaw Reid wrote the painter Edwin Austin Abbey (1852–1911), who was then living in England, asking him to prepare a painting 8 feet 7 inches by 3 feet 4 inches for the mantel over the fireplace in the dining room. The painting, "A Pavanne,"[88] was exhibited in the spring show of the National Academy of Design in 1897 before it was installed in the Reid house. In commissioning Abbey, Reid was following the example of Charles McKim, who had requested the painter to prepare panels for "The Quest for the Holy Grail" in 1893 for the Boston Public Library.

In 1904 the Reids decided they needed more service areas to facilitate entertaining, so a basement extension was built behind the house. It was under the right-of-way lot between 451 Madison and neighboring houses to the east. The Reids had the basement built by Louis Thouvard, a relatively minor New York architect. Thouvard ambitiously presented the Reids with a full set of drawings for a whitestone house in a Beaux-Arts style to sit upon the basement. The Reids did not commission the house but kept the drawings, and in 1910–1911 the new cellar space became the

Left: *The Reid dining room ca. 1900.* Opposite and below: *The breakfast room ca. 1910.* (*Museum of the City of New York.*)

Below: *Study for the façade of a house Louis Thouvard proposed ca. 1903–1904 for the lot at the rear of the south wing. Right: McKim, Mead & White plans for alterations to the basement and principal floors and for the 1910–1911 tower extension. (The New-York Historical Society.) Opposite: The renovations and tower addition in progress. (Museum of the City of New York.)*

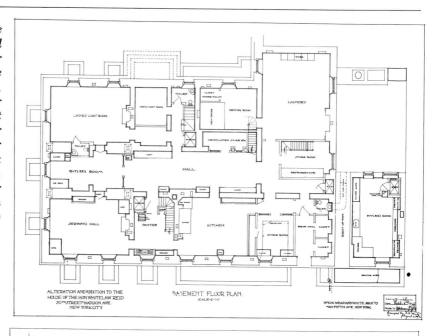

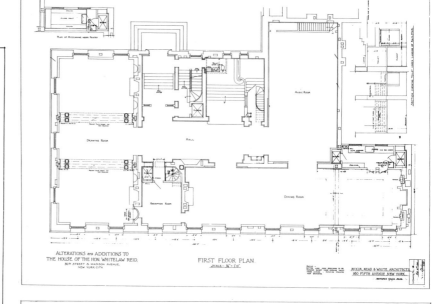

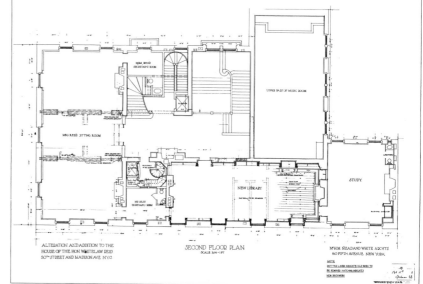

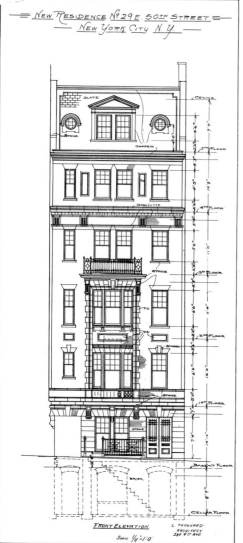

M. REID & CO.
BUILDERS
114-118 West 39TH ST.

PRINCE
IRON WORKS
STEEL CONSTRUCTION

M. REID & CO.
BUILDERS & CONTR
114-118 WES

Whitelaw Reid's library. (Museum of the City of New York.) Right: Library ceiling rondel painted by George Breck. (Avery Library.)

base of a tower addition designed by William Kendall of McKim, Mead & White. The tower was Renaissance in style and of the same Belleville brownstone as the house. (By this time, McKim and White were no longer alive. Stanford White died in 1906 and McKim in 1909, at Box Hill, in St. James, Long Island, the home of Stanford White's widow.)

The new tower made available an extra twenty feet to the rooms adjoining it. The dining room was extended into the new wing. The fireplace with its Saint-Gaudens reliefs and dolphin niches was moved twenty feet back to the east wall of the tower. Great care was taken to make the two sections blend harmoniously. An elaborate series of drawings, including large-scale renderings of details, was made. Even the German and Latin mottoes were appropriately duplicated in the new space.

At this time the Reids also created a new library on the second floor out of what had been two Villard guest rooms. These, according to a contemporary account of 1887,[89] were already in use as a library by Reid, but eventually further changes were deemed to be in order. A pair of Italian marble mantels were placed at each end of the library, and the room was filled with fine pieces of sixteenth-century Italian furniture. A door to the right of the fireplace led to a private study in the tower. The shallow barrel-vaulted plaster ceiling is embellished with coffers in low relief. The design alternates decorative rosettes with the colophons of famous publishing houses, very likely inspired by the inlays in the bookcase door details of Villard's library. Three large round paintings on canvas by George W. Breck (1853–1920) form part of the ceiling decoration. This room is still substantially intact.

A series of studies for planting and repaving the courtyard was done by McKim, Mead & White between 1911 and 1913. The final one retained the original brownstone gate posts and the distinctive wrought-iron arch and Renaissance-style lantern which have become so familiar to New Yorkers.

The Reids used their house for entertaining in the grand manner, and after completion of the tower addition in 1911, it was possible to do so on an even larger scale.

The house was sumptuous enough to make a handsome setting for a ball held on January 23, 1912, for Arthur, Duke of Connaught, third son of Britain's Queen Victoria, and his family. The duke, who was governor-general of Canada, made a special trip to New York at the invitation of the Reids. To underscore the private nature of the duke's visit to New York, no public events were held, but the ball was reported in the newspapers. Shortly thereafter Reid returned to his ambassadorial post in London, where he died later in the year. After his death Mrs. Reid continued to live in the New York house, to work for humanitarian causes and to entertain, when the occasion demanded it, in great style.

The swan song of splendid private parties at the Reid house was the ball on November 19, 1919, for Edward Albert, Prince of Wales. With the ending of the Great War, the era of lavish entertaining in New York began to draw to a close. A dinner at the William Henry Vanderbilt house, given by Mr. and Mrs. Cornelius Vanderbilt III, preceded the ball. The prince and his entourage arrived at ten-thirty at the Reid house, where they were received in the drawing room by Mrs. Reid and her daughter, Lady Ward, entertained by two orchestras, and greeted by several hundred guests, including General John J. Pershing, former President William Howard Taft, a suitable collection of Astors, Beekmans, Goelets, De Lanceys, Rockefellers, and Vanderbilts, and Governor Alfred E. Smith and Nicholas and Alice Roosevelt Longworth.

In the 1920s Mrs. Reid and her family began to spend more of their time at Ophir Hall, and after Mrs. Reid's death in 1931, the house at 451 Madison Avenue was closed. Furniture from there and from Ophir Hall was auctioned off in May 1935. The Edward Austin Abbey painting from the dining room went to the Metropolitan Museum of Art. The private residential life of the house had come to an end fifty years after it began.

VIII

New Neighbors

 s the fashionable residential neighborhoods in Manhattan moved uptown, the Villard houses had become an anachronistic symbol of nineteenth-century New York. Located in a prominent midtown position, yet gradually dwarfed by the large hotels, apartment houses, and office buildings that surrounded them, the dark brownstone houses conjured up an image of past grandeur. In the 1930 film *Holiday* Ann Harding is driven around the central courtyard of the Villard complex, gazing transfixed while exclaiming that the houses "looked like Pennsylvania Station." It was not intended as a comment on a common architectural origin; it was their imposing size and majestic presence that impressed the character in the movie. And of course, it was their size—the design for living on a grand scale—that made the expense of maintaining them as a private residence prohibitive in the postwar era. The day when one could hire servants to sleep in the attic and sweep, dust, and polish all day long for a few dollars a month was long over. The formal households for which these elegant and cosmopolitan town houses were designed no longer existed.

After the owners of the north and south wings died, the two largest houses remained closed and empty until World War II. Both were then reopened for the use of war-related organizations. The Villard-Reid residence became the Women's Military Service Club rest center. The Friends of Free France occupied the Fahnestock wing.

By the end of the war it was apparent to all that the days of private occupancy were past. A suggestion was made to turn the splendid rooms of 451 Madison Avenue into an interim site for the United Nations, but this came to nothing. Several other plans were proposed for adapting the houses to commercial or diplomatic use, but the rooms remained untenanted until 1946, when the combined Harris C. and William Fahnestock houses were purchased by the book publishers Random House, Inc. The late Bennett Cerf recounts in his posthumously published autobiography, *At Random,* the story of the acquisition of the house. After the Fahnestock heirs decided the house was too large to be retained as a residence, it was sold to a speculator and thence to the late Ambassador Joseph P. Kennedy, who bought it as an investment. As Cerf tells it, he had told a certain monsignor at St. Patrick's that he was looking for new quarters and was advised that the former Fahnestock house might be available. Cerf protested that the firm could not afford to buy such an expensive property but was assured that Kennedy could be induced to sell the house for the same amount he

Opposite: *St. Patrick's Cathedral from the complex, ca. 1941. (Courtesy Mrs. John G. Winslow.)*

The Villard/Reid house during occupancy by The Archdiocese of New York. Above: Conference room of the Metropolitan Tribunal, *the former drawing room, with Galland's panels still upon the walls.* Right: *The grand stair. A portion of the central portico is visible through the beveled plate-glass windows. (Photograph © Cervin Robinson.)* Opposite: *The Diocesan Consultors met in the Gold Room.*

had paid for it. The deal was arranged over the telephone, pressuring a presumably reluctant but unprotesting Kennedy to sell the house to the publishing company for $420,000.[90] It makes an excellent story, but a perusal of New York City Conveyances reveals that Kennedy actually had paid only $170,010 for the house a year and a half earlier.

At first the house was large enough for the publishing company, but as years went by, expansion of the company's operations brought about the division of formerly elegant interiors without regard for subtle details. Many decorative elements, including fireplaces and paneling, were greatly modified or disappeared in the process. Ceilings were dropped, and new openings cut in the walls. Temporary partitions, exposed lighting, and surface air-conditioning ducts were installed in a manner that seemed like a three-dimensional pun on the company's name.

Random House remained in the Villard complex until 1969, when its operations were moved to a new office tower on Third Avenue. Bennett Cerf always regretted the decision to leave. He felt the house should have been retained for the company's executive offices and swore that he would never leave voluntarily and would have to be carried out. When the time came to go, the scene was jokingly staged for photographers, and Cerf was carried out in a chair hefted by his associates.

Random House had taken over the front part of the north wing in 1946, but the south wing remained empty until 1948, when the Archbishopric of New York decided to reinvest in the site it had sold sixty-six years before. Francis Cardinal Spellman had only to look out of the windows of his residence to appreciate the convenience of locating the archdiocesan administrative offices in so dignified a setting just across the avenue.

The archbishopric first purchased the Villard-Reid house at 451 Madison Avenue and the Holmes house at No. 453. The following year the church acquired 455 Madison and the Roswell Smith house, 24 East 51st Street, and the adjoining lot at No. 26 from the Fahnestock family.

The architecture firm of Voorhees, Walker, Foley, & Smith was hired to make studies to convert all the properties the church had acquired into office space. Fortunately no comprehensive scheme was ever carried out; a benign neglect of the plans saved the majority of the most interesting interiors from extinction. The Adams house at No. 455 was never used as office space; it was kept as a residence for members of the clergy who worked in the administrative offices. Following the death of Mrs. Hubbard, the house at the rear of the north wing, 24 East 51st Street, was leased to Capital Cities Communications, Inc.

The archdiocese did make use of Nos. 451 and 453 as office space. The architects who had made the study were retained to make minimal changes in the major rooms of the principal floors at No. 451. The modifications were done with a respect for the character and detail of the original interiors and, in many cases, amounted to little more than the installation of adequate lighting fixtures to supplement the wall sconces and crystal chandeliers.

On the first floor of the Villard-Reid residence, the archdiocese converted the Gold Room into a conference chamber for the Diocesan Consultors. The Reid reception room facing Madison Avenue became a conference room for the Metropolitan Tribunal of the Archdiocese, and the dining room became the tribunal's courtroom. Some of the more hearty tributes to conviviality inscribed on the paneling were covered with strips of flexible wall-covering material, chaste architectural Band-Aids less in conflict with the spirit of tribunal proceedings. Whitelaw Reid's library became the chancery office, and his former study the office of the vicar-general of the Archdiocese. Work space for the secretarial staff of the chancery office was found in the Reid sitting rooms. The third and fourth floors were occupied by the Archdiocesan Building Commission, the Family Life Bureau, and the Institutional Commodity Services.

The house at No. 453, which never had had very elaborate interiors, was drastically renovated to provide modern office space for chancery agencies. Renamed the Cardinal Farley Building, it sheltered the Archdiocesan Service Corporation, the Alfred E. Smith Foundation, and the coordinator of Spanish Catholic Action on the principal floor. The upper floors contained the offices of the Society for the Propagation of the Faith, the Legion of Decency, and the Office for Radio and Television as well as the War Relief Services. At the rear, a modern extension was built to house a cafeteria.

The archbishopric also purchased the neighboring house, 31 East 50th Street, one of two by the architect Charles Coolidge Haight which predated the Reid tower addition, for the offices of the Confraternity of Christian Doctrine, the Secretary for Education, the Superintendent of Schools, and the Catholic Teachers Association.

The house at 30 East 51st Street which had been the home of Gibson Fahnestock was also acquired for the archdiocese and renamed the Cardinal Hayes Building. The Military Ordinariate was housed there.

Although the archdiocese owned the Roswell Smith house, such postwar interior renovations as were done there were carried out for Capital Cities Communications. Here again, the significant residential character was retained on the principal floor. The appearance of this house today seems to conform to what we know of the Babb, Cook & Willard renovations of 1886 from records, including the rough sketch which accompanied the Building Department applications. No detailed early plans have been located, but it is clear that the present layout is different from the plan published in the McKim, Mead & White monograph.

Lowell Thomas, who is a principal of Capital Cities Communications, established the drawing room as the location for the mementos of his long career as a broadcaster and journalist, covering the walls with photographs of his expeditions and adventures. Bookcases installed along one wall held red leather-bound volumes of the transcripts of his radio broadcasts.

In the course of the various remodelings by Capital Cities, the paneling and wainscot, particularly in the entrance area reception room and stair hall, were removed and reworked in order to conceal various modern wiring, air-conditioning, and lighting systems. Some of the paneling and wainscot details appear to have been rearranged or slightly modified in the process. This further complicates the attribution of the interior, making it nearly impossible to distinguish what may have survived from McKim, Mead & White's designs for the original construction from what may have been done by Babb, Cook & Willard for Roswell Smith.

Headquarters of Capital Cities Communications, 24 East 51st Street, in 1977. Left: The office of Lowell Thomas. The paneled door and overmantel are from the original interior. Below: First floor landing. The staircase and paneling are part of Babb, Cook & Willard's 1886 interiors for Roswell Smith. (Photographs © Cervin Robinson.)

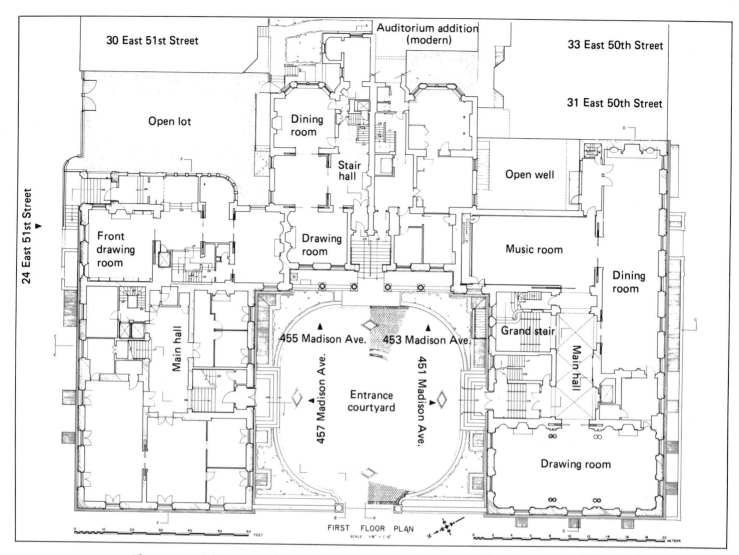

30 East 51st Street

Auditorium addition (modern)

33 East 50th Street

31 East 50th Street

Open lot

Dining room

Stair hall

Open well

24 East 51st Street

Front drawing room

Drawing room

Music room

Dining room

Main hall

Grand stair

Main hall

455 Madison Ave.

453 Madison Ave.

457 Madison Ave.

451 Madison Ave.

Entrance courtyard

Drawing room

FIRST FLOOR PLAN
SCALE: 1/8" = 1'-0"

0 10 20 30 40 50 60 FEET

0 2 4 6 8 10 12 14 16 18 20 METERS

This measured drawing of the first floor made in 1978 for the Historic American Buildings Survey reveals the scope of the changes from the original McKim, Mead & White plan and later changes, including the Reid tower, the Adams rear extension, and the Roswell Smith portico and entry. (Drawing by Alan Soller, courtesy Emery Roth & Sons.) Right: View northwest from the now-vanished Reid tower, winter 1977. The rear ridge line of the house, running diagonally across the picture, is clearly visible against the snow. Along this line the formal brownstone façade gave way to plain brick at the rear of the complex. All portions to the right of this line have been demolished. (Photograph © Cervin Robinson.)

IX

Preparing for the Second Century

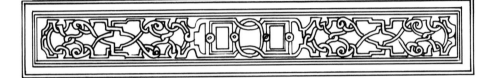

n the three decades following World War II, much had altered in the immediate neighborhood of the Villard houses. The changes began with such architecturally distinguished modern office structures as Lever House and the Seagram Building. Soon Park Avenue above the former New York Central Office Building (now the Helmsley Building) was transformed from its sedate elegance as a neighborhood of apartment houses, hotels, and clubs to one of skyscrapers housing the home offices of America's corporate giants. The New Weston Hotel at 50th Street and Madison Avenue, with its traditional English Grill Room and high tea served in the lobby, was demolished in the late 1960s to make way for the ITT tower and its small plaza. Virtually all of Park Avenue, from 46th Street to 57th Street, traded its uniform brick and limestone façades for a sheath of glass-curtain-walled commercial towers. Now only the Racquet Club, St. Bartholomew's Church, and the Waldorf-Astoria bore witness to the former character of the area.[91]

Many New Yorkers were appalled by the rapid changes taking place in the city and the loss of prominent structures such as Pennsylvania Station, the Singer Building, and the old Metropolitan Opera House.[92] In 1965, at the end of Mayor Robert Wagner's administration, the New York City Landmarks Preservation Commission was established in an attempt to deal with the problem.

Despite the original grave reservations of the conservative real estate establishment, the popular appeal of preservation in a city which bore the scars of a decade of urban renewal gradually brought about a general perception that historic preservation could be a stabilizing factor in the revitalization of urban neighborhoods, and the Landmarks Commission grew enormously in prestige and influence during the administration (1966–1974) of Mayor John V. Lindsay.

The legislation establishing the commission provided for six-month designation periods during which public hearings could be held and additional buildings designated for landmark status, alternating with three-year moratoriums during which no further buildings could be designated. During these long intervals architecturally significant structures were sometimes threatened with demolition, and no legal means existed to prevent irreversible losses.

In 1973, close to the end of his term, Mayor Lindsay introduced several amendments to the original landmarks law which considerably increased the commission's ability to cope with the pressures of change so characteristic of New York.

The new provisions eliminated the three-year limitation on designation hearings and included the ability to designate significant publicly accessible interiors (churches and clubs were excluded because of constitutional requirements) and scenic landmarks, such as monuments, parks, and landscape features, as well as public accountability for city-owned landmarks, including firehouses, court buildings, and police headquarters.

The complexity of the issues involved in the long process of adapting the Villard houses to New York's contemporary realities and preparing them for their second century can be understood only in the context of this background.

During the heady optimism of the 1960s New York's boom and prosperity seemed boundless. Midtown real estate values soared, reaching unprecedented levels as commercial tenants grabbed any available space, regardless of price, to provide for business expansion. Faced with rising costs of maintenance and the aging physical plant of its own extensive network of religious, educational, and institutional properties, the archdiocese of New York sought to consolidate in one new building the services housed in several of its midtown institutional properties. This released some of the most valuable sites for commercial development.

After the departure of Random House in 1969, its quarters in the Villard complex had remained on the market until 1971. In that year Henry J. Gaisman donated $2,250,000 so that the archbishopric could purchase the north wing and complete the assemblage of a plot large enough for new development.

The changing character of the neighborhood adjacent to the Queensboro Bridge had led to a diminishing use of St. John's Church at 55th Street (the same parish which had once had its church on the Villard houses site). The building at 55th Street was demolished, and in its place was built a contemporary twenty-story tower, the Catholic Center, which brought together under one roof a new St. John's Church, the administrative offices of the archdiocese, and the Cathedral Girls' High School. (The school had been housed in a nondescript neo-Gothic 1920s structure at Lexington Avenue and 50th Street, adjacent to the Byzantine-Romanesque St. Bartholomew's Parish House and the Art Deco General Electric Building.[93])

No sooner had the archdiocese moved from the Villard houses and into the new Catholic Center in 1973 than the real estate boom collapsed and New York was plunged into the worst recession since the crash of 1929. The development company which had been scheduled to construct an office building on the Cathedral Girls' High School site dropped its plans, and the building was finally leased to the City University system. The Villard houses now sat vacant, with Capital Cities Communications as the only occupant. Church property which is not used for religious, educational, or charitable purposes over a period of two years is returned to the tax rolls, and the archbishopric was now obliged to pay annual taxes in excess of $700,000. Many commercial, public, and cultural uses were proposed. None of these plans succeeded, and the houses remained closed, visited only by an occasional postman, delivery boy, or visitor seeking Random House or the Chancery. An elaborate and patiently planned real estate program was foundering in the depressed real estate market, but attempts to find occupants for the vacant space in the houses continued. An elaborate rental brochure was devised in the hope of attracting tenants for the complex and the church-owned houses behind it.

In the midst of this predicament, the church fathers were relieved when, in the spring of 1974, a major New York realtor, Harry B. Helmsley, offered to lease the Villard houses and the adjacent properties for commercial development as a combined office, hotel, and apartment structure. Others, however, were less happy about the proposal. Preservationists were doubtful that the elaborate interiors and historic details of the landmark façades would get the attention they deserved, and efforts were made to halt the project.

Helmsley had chosen as his architects Emery Roth & Sons, a firm that has often been engaged as consultants or associates to design-oriented architectural firms in the realization of such buildings as the World Trade Center, the Pan Am Building, the General Motors Building, and the Citicorp Center.[94]

Their credentials did nothing to soothe the concerns of historic preservationists, for the architects' early design studies called for the demolition of the celebrated Gold Room and the 1910 tower addition, which contained the marble dining-room fireplace wall designed by Stanford White and Augustus Saint-Gaudens and Whitelaw Reid's wood-marquetry-paneled study.

Many critics felt that as room was made for lobbies, restaurants, and ballrooms of the new building and the flanking wings were turned to unspecified commercial uses, the remaining portion of the central courtyard façade would be reduced to a meaningless stage set. Some feared that once the new tower was constructed, the older structures would be demolished for a plaza.

The complex arrangements for leasing the site to the developer extend into the middle of the next century. They provide a number of legal safeguards for the treatment of the landmark exteriors of the Villard houses, but the actual design of the new buildings and the use and treatment of the interiors of the old ones was the developer's responsibility. His participation in turn was conditional on the archbishopric's obtaining the necessary official zoning permissions and approvals for a combined hotel, apartment, and office tower. This set the stage for a protracted public debate which was to delay the project for several years.

Preservationists and members of the surrounding community enlisted the support of professional and civic groups, public officials, elected representatives, and press, and anyone else they could rally to the cause. They eventually succeeded in persuading the New York City planning agencies to accept protection of the significant interiors as a condition of approval for any variance, but the process took three years and involved more than seventy-five official meetings and fifteen public hearings.

In January 1976 the archdiocese sought assistance in allaying the concerns of preservationists and engaged one of the authors of this book, William C. Shopsin, AIA, as historic preservation consultant to the project, charging him with the responsibility of making a historic survey and of consulting with all the parties with a view to resolving the conflicts.

The preservation problems of the Villard houses, although perhaps unique in New York, are not unusual when understood in terms of the larger context of efforts and procedures common in Europe for more than a century—practices which are rapidly becoming more widely accepted in the United States.

The technical feasibility of adapting the Villard houses to new uses was never in doubt. The Chancery of the Archdiocese, Random House, and Capital Cities Communications all had functioned successfully within the complex for decades.

But with the changes in the needs of its occupants the Villard houses complex, although still structurally sound and basically in good repair, had become functionally obsolete again. Turn-of-the-century nonfireproof construction methods and materials, plumbing, climatization, elevators, and electrical wiring were not up to modern standards and were in need of considerable reworking.

Not all old buildings can be transformed into museums. Much of the vitality of an original building is lost when it is isolated from the mainstream of its community and surroundings. But it seemed obvious that any contemporary use of the Villard houses complex, even if unburdened by real estate taxes, would never be able to generate the revenues necessary to revitalize the structures. Some additional source of revenue was necessary in order to justify the heavy investment to bring the existing structures back into use. Fortunately, the foresight of the archbishopric in creating a large enough plot assemblage made it possible to retain the principal portions of the Villard houses façades yet construct a new major revenue-producing structure on the site as well.

The primary role of a historic preservation consultant in the context of such a project is to assist the developer, his architect, engineers, and contractors in achieving a sensitive and appropriate transition between the old buildings and the new structure. Foremost in these considerations is the protection of the integrity of both the interior and the exterior of the historic structure during the long and complicated process of major construction under the congested conditions of midtown Manhattan. But most new construction in New York City goes up in close proximity to existing buildings which must continue to function throughout the entire process, and appropriate safeguards must always be made for their structural integrity. Once a thorough historic survey was completed, detailed construction preparations could get under way.

Careful measurements, detailed photographs, inventories of special hardware, lighting fixtures, railings, special decorative elements, locations of fragile interior finishes all were essential. Since many of these items would have been very expensive, if not impossible, to repair or replace, special preparations were made to protect some things *in situ*. Others were removed to safe storage, to be replaced at the completion of the adjacent new construction and after restoration work within the old portions of the complex was finished.

Parallel with the process of documentation for the survey was the development of an elaborate strategy for the protection of the houses during the construction of the adjacent fifty-one-story new Palace hotel tower. Some of the rear extensions had to come down in order to link the Villard houses to the new hotel, and an investigation of the original construction to see how far this should go revealed something many ordinary pedestrians had never observed. Seen from Madison Avenue, the sloping terra-cotta tile roofs of the houses gave the impression that they enclosed a full attic story. In fact, the roof rose only to the main ridgeline; the rear portions of the central houses had shallow pitched roofs and raised brick parapet walls, and the back walls of the wings reached the ridgeline. The entire elevation facing east to the rear yard was, in fact, meant to be concealed from view and therefore had no "architectural façade treatment."

The Landmarks Preservation Commission therefore established the ridgeline of the roof 100 feet east of Madison Avenue as the limit of the exterior landmark designation. This meant that the rear extensions and later accretions built beyond that line could be demolished to make room for the base of the new hotel.

One of the aims of the survey was to provide historical data for reference and study once the actual rooms were dismantled, a guide for their reassembly and reconstruction either within the new hotel or elsewhere.

It would also provide the basis for the development of the detailed plans and specifications for the restoration of the Villard houses complex itself. This was a most important part of the survey, for the final agreement that had been arrived at over so many months among the many parties involved rested on an understanding that major portions of the interiors would be faithfully restored to their earlier condition.

The initial approach of the survey was to try to sort out the most historic and architecturally significant features of the Villard houses, particularly the interiors. These had not been included in the original designation because interiors were not provided for in the initial New York City landmarks legislation. The fate of the interiors was, however, the principal cause of concern to most critics of the project, and it became evident that a solution would have to be arrived at through separate agreements.

Trying to sort out the significant interiors from the more ordinary and functional rooms, cellars, attics, and closets was not easy. Many of the project's staunchest critics had claimed that every

Measured drawings from the HAB Survey. Above: Rear elevation. The center portion shows the Holmes and Adams dwellings sharing a common pediment. At right is the Roswell Smith portico and extension. Drawn by Weerapan Wattanavijarn. Left: South elevation of the Fahnestock wing and longitudinal section of the Adams/Michalis house. Drawn by Kun-Hyuck Ahn. (Courtesy Emery Roth & Sons.)

EAST 50th STREET

EAST 51st STREET

MADISON AVENUE

square inch of the houses was exquisite and inviolate. But some parts had never been particularly distinguished and had already been altered more than once, and it was possible to concede that the majority of the interiors could be utilized for institutional, hotel, or commercial purposes with no loss to posterity.

A main focus of the opposition to the project was the zoning aspects and the precedent it might set for enlargement of other landmark sites. The intricacies of the bulk and size formulas of the New York City codes are not easily comprehended by the uninitiated. Thus the necessity for obtaining a special permit was not fully understood by many critics who regarded any bonus a giveaway. Fundamentally the need for special legislation was caused by the retention of the landmark houses. This forced the crowding of the new hotel-apartment tower onto only half the total 200-by-200-foot site.

Ordinarily this would have been a perfectly adequate site for commercial development, but in order to accommodate all the lobbies, service loading docks, garage entries, and accessory functions as well as to retain the Villard houses, the only ground left uncovered was the original courtyard. Under the present New York City zoning code standards for open plazas, this was considered inadequate. Eventually an exception was made which substituted for a larger plaza the amenity of the ground floor lobby's use as a pedestrian through-block arcade linking the 51st Street and 50th Street entrances, via a grand stair, to the Madison Avenue courtyard entrance.

But much more serious statutory problems remained to be resolved. New York City law assigns the responsibility for new construction to the City Planning Commission and for preservation of the old to the Landmarks Preservation Commission. The construction of a fifty-one-story tower behind a five-story landmark brought both city agencies into a partnership that was never envisioned by those who had drafted the respective enabling legislation. The resultant relationship could best be described as a marriage not made in heaven.

Negotiations among the representatives of all the parties involved usually required a fair-sized conference table. But a final preservation plan was at last drafted by the attorneys, principally by Kevin McGrath representing the archbishopric, Dorothy Miner for the Landmarks Commission, and Norman Marcus for the City Planning Commission.[95] The process was characterized by innumerable drafts and redrafts, interminable conferences, public hearings, and statements to the press.

The public relations campaign, including private persuasion efforts to win support for the project, was an enormous task. The Villard houses development had stirred up latent anticlerical as well as antilandlord sentiments (as the city's largest residential as well as commercial real estate management firm, the Helmsley organization had quite a following of its own), and a great deal of anger and frustration found its outlet on more than one occasion. Nevertheless, by the autumn of 1977 serious planning was under way, although several hurdles remained to be cleared before the actual construction was finally begun on March 14, 1978, four years after Helmsley's offer to the archdiocese.

As a result of the elaborate preservation agreements negotiated as part of the special enabling legislation, the patient and meticulous process of measuring, recording, and documenting the houses for the Historic American Building Survey had to be undertaken.

James Rhodes, a young architect who had recently supervised the restoration and adaptation of Andrew Carnegie's Fifth Avenue mansion for the Cooper-Hewitt-Smithsonian Museum of Design for Hardy Holzman Pfeiffer Associates, was hired by Helmsley's architects, Emery Roth & Sons, as project manager for this phase of the project.

Rhodes assembled a team in the Roth office. They had never before attempted such an effort, but in the end they produced what is probably the most exhaustive and elaborate set of measured drawings since the establishment in 1934 of the Historic American Buildings Survey as a program of the NRA to put unemployed architects back to work. These superb drawings are now part of the HABS permanent archives in the United States Library of Congress.

(An article in the Home Section of the *New York Times* on December 27, 1979, noted that two enterprising architects have selected from the HABS archives a sampling of plans with the intention of reproducing them and making them available by mail to people who want to reproduce period houses on their own lots. It seems unlikely that anyone would try to duplicate Henry Villard's palace in his own backyard, but given the revisionism of today's postmodern architects, one can never be too certain. After a long period of neglect and disparagement by the architectural establishment, the works of McKim, Mead & White and others of their generation have been experiencing a tremendous revival of interest. The "Ecole des Beaux Arts" exhibition at the Museum of Modern Art in 1975 and the Brooklyn Museum's "Renaissance in American Architecture" show in 1979 have brought about a new appreciation of this cultural legacy and its part in the development of a distinctive American tradition in architecture and the decorative arts.)

Houses and hotel were to abut one another. The construction of any tall tower in New York means blasting deep into bedrock. It was therefore essential to plan a careful sequence of demolition so that fragile parquet, mosaic inlays, and marble floors were not scratched or damaged. Wood paneling, marquetry work, stained glass, and decorated plaster had to be shielded from excessive vibration as well as abrasion. The same specialists who monitored the construction of the new additions to the Metropolitan Museum of Art were engaged to supervise the work. All visible cracks or defects on the exterior and interior were examined and photographed. Special shoring was installed to strengthen the houses while construction was in progress. Seismographs were strategically placed to record minute changes in vibration as drilling, blasting, and demolition progressed. When seismographs trembled, construction stopped.

Certainly in these respects the Villard–Palace hotel project set an innovative and extraordinary precedent for a New York City commercial construction project. The protracted negotiations, at first so frustrating, gradually brought about a greater appreciation of the unique potential which the *fin-de-siècle* interiors offered. The developer, his architects, interior designers, and management teams undertook a total reuse scheme which restores all the most significant spaces in the Villard complex to elegant and appropriate uses. The plans of the principal floors of the combined Villard houses and new hotel spaces indicates the ingenious fashion in which complex functional requirements have been maneuvered to fit the existing configurations and still respect the architectural integrity envisioned by its original designers.

At the end of this long and bumpy voyage most of the original design team was intact, with Richard Roth, Jr., of Emery Roth & Sons still at the helm. Many more specialists and consultants were now to be brought in to produce the design, working drawings, and specifications for the project.

During the depressed mood of the late 1970s recession and the city's severe fiscal plight, the banks and insurance companies financing the project had already forced Helmsley to eliminate the proposed office floors from the tower. This reduction in the height of the tower simplified the architects' task of organizing the complex functional requirements being squeezed into the limited configuration imposed by retention of the Villard houses on half the available site. The elimination of a separate office building lobby on the ground floor eased the circulation patterns and made possible the single through-block lobby arcade linking 51st Street and 50th Street.

Thus the most difficult task was to decide how to adapt and reuse the historic portions of the Villard houses. All the significant spaces selected by the Landmarks Preservation Commission were located on the first and second floors of the Villard houses and in effect represented perhaps only 20 percent of their total floor space.

*The Villard houses undergoing restoration, April 1980. (M.V.)
Below: Plan showing how interior spaces of the complex have been incorporated with the new hotel. The floor designation represents the hotel level. The second floor of The Palace is one-half-story above the parlor floor of the landmark structure. (Courtesy Emery Roth & Sons.)*

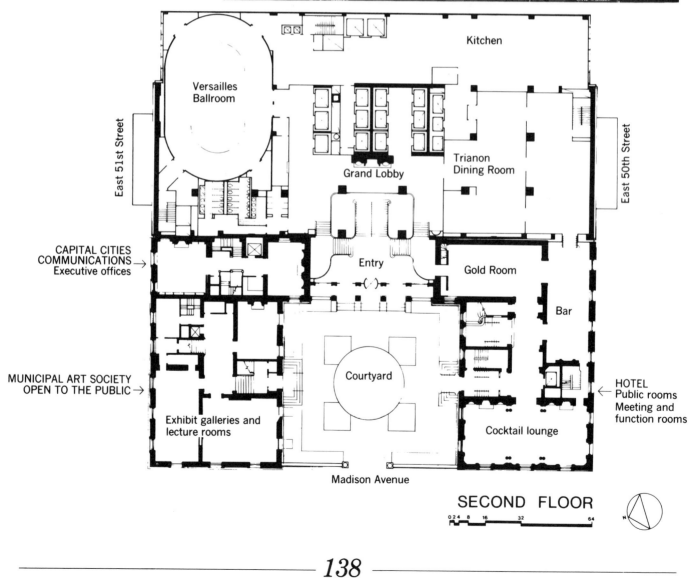

Kitchen

Versailles Ballroom

East 51st Street

East 50th Street

Grand Lobby

Trianon Dining Room

CAPITAL CITIES COMMUNICATIONS
Executive offices →

Entry

Gold Room

Bar

MUNICIPAL ART SOCIETY OPEN TO THE PUBLIC →

Courtyard

HOTEL
← Public rooms
Meeting and function rooms

Exhibit galleries and lecture rooms

Cocktail lounge

Madison Avenue

SECOND FLOOR

0 2 4 8   16   32   64

N

Upon closer study, it turned out that the greatest restrictions were imposed not by the preservation of specific interiors, but rather by the original construction of the houses themselves. Because the houses were built mostly of solid masonry-bearing brick faced on the exterior with brownstone, it became readily apparent that any major attempts to shift layouts to suit commercial tenants would be costly and impractical. It also became clear that the potential users would have to adapt themselves to the houses rather than the other way around. Once this operating principle was established, it became easier to justify economically the retention and restoration of many more decorative features throughout the houses than were originally envisaged or required by the preservation agreements.

The first commitment to move into the houses came from Capital Cities Communications, which was anxious to retain its old quarters in 24 East 51st Street, but needed more space. It has, therefore, expanded into the upper portions of the two central houses, 455 and 453 Madison, in the space above the arcaded entrances leading from the courtyard to the hotel as well as into the upper floors of 451 Madison, the old Villard-Whitelaw Reid wing. The elaborate arrangements incorporate and preserve as much as possible of the original decorative elements.

As the plans reveal, the spatial reorganization of the Villard houses is quite complex. The hotel occupies the lower floors of the Villard-Whitelaw Reid wing. The basement serves as the "below stairs" or, more correctly, "back of the house" space for management and administrative functions, and the Villard's former service entrance on 50th Street is now a personnel entrance.

On the main floor, all the principal rooms, including the Gold Room, have been restored to their former glory and function as the public rooms, lobbies, and lounges of the hotel. Whitelaw Reid's library and drawing room on the second floor have been restored as meeting rooms with a service pantry for private dining. Reid's tower study (later Cardinal Spellman's office) has been reconstructed on the third floor of the new hotel as a meeting room, along with Edward Dean Adams's study from 455 Madison Avenue.

The Saint-Gaudens fireplace wall from the former dining room has been relocated as the focal point of the new hotel lobby and is seen on axis from Madison Avenue, through the courtyard and the glazed arcaded entrances. The new courtyard hotel entry brings one to the mid-level landing of a new monumental marble stair linking the restaurant, cocktail lounge, and ballroom above with the main desk, check-in facilities, and street-level through-block lobby below.

Perhaps the most engaging note, considering the long struggle to preserve the houses, is the adaptation of the north wing, 457 Madison Avenue, as The Urban Center. There The Municipal Art Society of New York, the Parks Council, the Architectural League, and the New York Chapter of the American Institute of Architects now have their headquarters and share in the programming of events in the public spaces. The creation of the Center was initiated by The Municipal Art Society, which leased the wing, invited the other organizations to participate, and rented some of the space to commercial tenants to help make the venture financially self-supporting. In the elegant parlor floor reception rooms that Charles Platt designed for William Fahnestock, visitors now browse among the books on architecture and historic preservation in the publications center, view exhibitions, and attend lectures and seminars on landmark preservation and urban art and architecture. They also make use of The Information Exchange, a referral and information service on urban design operated by The Municipal Art Society.

Thus has the long debate about the fate of the Villard houses resulted at last in a creative marriage between preservation and development, an encouraging conclusion to a difficult chapter in their history, and a promising beginning for their second century.

Notes

Prologue

    1. Charles Lockwood, *Bricks & Brownstone* (New York: 1972), p. 42.

    2. Quoted in New York City Landmarks Preservation Commission, *Greenwich Village Historic District Report* (New York: 1969), vol. I, p. 53.

    3. Eno Collection, No. 341 (Prints Division, New York Public Library).

    4. Ellen W. Kramer, "The Domestic Architecture of Detlef Lienau, A Conservative Victorian" (Ph.D. dissertation, New York University, 1957), p. 167. For Marble Row and the Colford Jones Block, see pp. 164–71. According to *Manufacturer and Builder* (February 1874), p. 33, "the marble entrances, the ornaments, and the details of the interiors" of the two houses at the 58th Street end of Marble Row had yet to be completed.

    5. According to Dennis S. Francis, who is an authority on the work of Calvert Vaux. Traditionally the date of the remodeling has been given as 1874.

    6. Jacob Landy, "The Domestic Architecture of the 'Robber Barons' in New York City," *Marsyas*, vol. 5 (1947–1949), pp. 69–71.

Chapters 1–9

A good many scholars have made contributions to the information contained in this book. Footnotes which list their names without citing documents indicate that the observation was verbal.

    1. *New York Times*, July 12, 1858, p. 8, quoted in Leland Cook, *St. Patrick's Cathedral* (New York, London, Tokyo: 1979), p. 55.

    2. John A. Kouwenhoven, *The Columbia Historical Portrait of New York* (New York: 1972), p. 347.

    3. George A. Kelly, *The Parish*, St. John's University (New York: 1973), pp. 36–37.

    4. *Real Estate Record and Guide*, vol. 28 (1881), p. 1146.

    5. Columbia University Manuscript Division, Hamilton Fish Collection.

    6. William H. Pierson, Jr. *American Buildings and Their Architects* (Garden City, N.Y.: 1978), p. 240 and pp. 265–68.

    7. "The New York House of the Future," *The Real Estate Record*, vol. 28 (December 1881), p. 1208. The cathedral casts a shadow on Villard's site and the setback around the courtyard makes the best use of the light, as his architects would have pointed out to him (Professor Sarah Bradford Landau).

    8. Oswald Garrison Villard, New York *Sun*, February 25, 1946.

    9. "The New York House of the Future," the Bromley and Robinson 1879 *Atlas of the City of New York* shows a structure which might have been a well or springhouse in the center of what would become Villard's courtyard. So convenient a water source would have encouraged placement of a fountain there.

    10. Henry-Russell Hitchcock. (For the Thurn and Taxis, see also Dr. Carl Wolff and Dr. Rudolf Jung, *Die*

Baudenkmäler in Frankfurt am Main, vol. 2 [Frankfurt: 1898], pp. 401ff.)

    11. The grounds at Thorwood may have been landscaped by Frederick Law Olmsted.

    12. Henry-Russell Hitchcock, *The Architecture of H. H. Richardson and His Times* (Cambridge, Mass.: 1979), p. 135 and pp. 156–58.

    13. *Ibid.*, pp. 139–40.

    14. Charles Moore, *The Life and Times of Charles Follen McKim* (Boston and New York: 1929), p. 46.

    15. Charles Baldwin, *Stanford White* (New York: 1971; reprint of the 1931 edition), pp. 357–58.

    16. H. M. Whidden, a draftsman in the McKim, Mead & White office, had worked with McKim on preparation of the designs for the hotel. Baldwin, *op. cit.*, footnote, p. 156.

    17. Wells claimed to be a direct descendant of Samuel Adams (Moore, p. 42, in a quote from Mead). Hence he may have been related to William V. Wells (1826–1876) of Boston, a great-grandson of Samuel Adams and author of *The Life and Public Services of Samuel Adams* (Boston: 1865), 3 vols.

    18. C. Howard Walker worked on the archaeological excavations at Assos in Turkey with Charles Eliot Norton and Francis Bacon in the late 1870s and early 1880s before setting up an architectural practice in Boston.

    19. C. Howard Walker, "Joseph Wells, Architect," *The Architectural Record*, vol. 66 (1929), pp. 15–16.

    20. Royal Contissoz, *Art and Common Sense* (New York: 1913), p. 421.

    21. Walker, *op. cit.*, p. 16.

    22. Homer Saint-Gaudens, *The Reminiscences of Augustus Saint-Gaudens* (New York: 1913), vol. 1, pp. 306–11.

    23. Baldwin, *op. cit.*, p. 357.

    24. *Ibid.*, pp. 361–63.

    25. *Ibid.*, pp. 364–65.

    26. Letter from Professor Leland Roth of September 5, 1979.

    27. Baldwin, *op. cit.*, footnote, p. 358. The only New York newspaper to publish as obituary of Wells was Villard's *Evening Post*.

    28. *Hitchcock, op. cit.*, p. 297.

    29. Mariana Griswold van Rensselaer, "City Residences," *Century Magazine*, vol. 31, no. 4 (February 1886), p. 550.

    30. Moore, *op. cit.*, p. 62.

    31. Wells designed the base for McKim, Mead & White (letter by Wells, Wendell P. Garrison Collection, Houghton Library, Harvard University). The sculptor of the statue, Olin Levi Warner (1844–1896), was a neighbor of Wells's in The Benedict, 80 Washington Square, an apartment house for bachelors designed by McKim, Mead, & White in 1879 and built between 1879 and 1882 (Wayne Craven, *Sculpture in America* [New York: 1968], pp. 407–408).

    32. Baldwin, *op. cit.*, p. 358.

    33. *Ibid.*, pp. 358–59.

    34. *Ibid.*, p. 359.

    35. Evarts, Choate and Beaman were patrons of

Saint-Gaudens and clients of McKim, Mead & White. For Choate, the architects built Naumkeag in Stockbridge, Massachusetts, in 1884–1887 and for Beaman, some cottages in Rockaway, Long Island, in 1881.

36. Baldwin, *op. cit.*, p. 359.

37. *Ibid.*, p. 356.

38. Walker, *op. cit.*, p. 18.

39. Baldwin, *op. cit.*, p. 360.

40. Walker, *op. cit.*, p. 18.

41. Baldwin, *op. cit.*, p. 363.

42. Louis C. Tiffany's sketch for the house is reproduced in Robert Koch, *Louis C. Tiffany, Rebel in Glass* (New York: 1974), p. 94.

43. Henry-Russell Hitchcock.

44. Moore, *op. cit.*, p. 48.

45. Post had no previous commission as a Vanderbilt architect. During the Civil War Post had served in the New York Twenty-second Regiment with David E. Gwynne, brother of Alice Gwynne (Mrs. Cornelius II) Vanderbilt. The introduction may have come through the Gwynnes.

46. Earl Shinn (Edward Strahan), *Mr. Vanderbilt's House and Collection*, Japan edition (Philadelphia: n.d.), p. 7.

47. John Vredenburgh Van Pelt, *A Monograph of the William K. Vanderbilt House* (New York: 1925), pp. 13–14.

48. Shinn, *op. cit.*, p. 7.

49. Wayne Andrews, *Architecture, Ambition and Americans* (New York: 1964), p. 179.

50. For the Fifth Avenue Hotel see the *Granite Monthly*, vol. X (1887), p. 317, for the attribution to Griffith Thomas. The article credits William Washburn with the interior. According to the Snook firm contract books at The New-York Historical Society, John B. Snook was apparently building at this corner at this time, making it seem that he was the contractor for the hotel.

51. Hitchcock, *op. cit.*, p. 54.

52. McKim, Mead & White Collection, The New-York Historical Society.

53. This story comes from Dee Brown, *Hear That Lonesome Whistle Blow* (New York: 1977), pp. 256–58.

54. New York *World*, January 5, 1884, p. 2.

55. New York *Herald*, January 3, 1884.

56. New York *Tribune*, January 4, 1884, and William M. Armstrong, *E. L. Godkin, A Biography* (Albany, N.Y.: 1978), p. 142.

57. Fanny Garrison Villard, ed., *Memoirs of Henry Villard* (Boston and New York: 1904), 2 vols.

58. Van Rensselaer, *op. cit.*, p. 557.

59. Villard and Holmes fell out over a case involving Judge Davis and the Northern Pacific Railroad. (Letter dated April 3, 1889, Villard Papers, Houghton Library, Harvard University.) Holmes ends: "It is likely to be a rivalry between Mrs. Holmes and [Mrs. Adams] . . . on the subject of baby carriages and their style and ornamentation. . . ." Edward Dean Adams's daughter was born a year after Lillian Holmes.

60. McKim first alone, then with his partners, built some dozen houses in this fashionable seaside community.

61. Shinn, *op. cit.*, p. 7.

62. Saint-Gaudens, *op. cit.*, 2, p. 362.

63. Francis Bacon has many connections to this tale. An early apprentice in the offices of McKim, Mead & White, he supported himself by working in architectural offices so that he could spend the summers at archaeological excavations in Assos, Turkey. Bacon designed furniture for H. H. Richardson between 1884 and 1885, then became chief designer for A. H. Davenport Company, a position he held for much of the rest of his life. He was also responsible for the interiors of 455 Madison Avenue, according to Ruth Adams (Mrs. Leighton) Lobdell, daughter of Edward Dean Adams, who reports that Bacon was a friend of the family.

64. One painting we can be sure was never in the house is "The Madonna delle Fiaccole or dei Candelabri" which was offered to Villard by Luigi Palma di Cesnola (1832–1904), the first director of the Metropolitan Museum of Art. In a letter to Villard dated July 25, 1883, General Cesnola described the painting, then on loan to the museum, as belonging to Henry Munro Butler Johnstone and said it was the first Raphael to cross the Atlantic. He suggested that "the possession of such a picture would make famous any private or public gallery in this country" and offered Villard this "gem" for his "new palatial house" with the observation that "there would be many jealous no doubt but you would possess the finest picture in America." Villard did not buy the picture, and it went back to England in 1884. The contents of the letter, which is now among the Villard Papers in the Houghton Library of Harvard University, is supplemented by information provided by Jeanie James-Rengstorff, associate archivist of the Metropolitan Museum of Art, in a letter of February 13, 1980.

65. A possible precedent for this vaulted hall with mosaiclike patterning is George Fletcher Babb's library ceiling for the C. T. Barney house at 10 East 55th Street, now demolished. The house was designed by McKim, Mead & White in 1880, but decorated by Babb, who did the library between 1881 and 1882.

66. *The Record and Guide* (November 14, 1885), p. 1247.

67. Craven, *op. cit.*, p. 377.

68. *Artistic Houses* (New York: 1883–1884; reprint, New York, 1971), p. 162.

69. Siena is the choice of marble in *The Record and Guide* (November 14, 1885), p. 1248, and *History of Architecture and Building Trades of Greater New York* (New York: 1899), vol. 2, p. 84, and Numidian marble is specified in *Artistic Houses, op. cit.*, p. 163.

70. *The Record and Guide* (November 14, 1885), p. 1248.

71. *Ibid.*

72. Anne Farnham, curator of the Essex Institute, Salem, Massachusetts.

73. Color descriptions vary. *The Record and Guide* (November 14, 1885), p. 1248, and *Artistic Houses, op. cit.*, p. 163.

74. *The Record and Guide* (November 14, 1885), p. 1248.

75. *Artistic houses, op. cit.*, p. 163.

76. *The Record and Guide*, p. 1248.

77. *Artistic Houses, op. cit.*, p. 163.

78. *Ibid.*

79. *The Record and Guide* (November 14, 1885), p. 1248.

80. *Ibid.*

81. McKim, Mead & White Collection, The New-York Historical Society. The charges probably related to work done on the vestibule of the Holmes portion of the central houses.

82. New York City Buildings Department Records. Alteration 1958, September 28, 1886, ". . . the interior has never been finished. . . ." Specifications for the addition are given.

83. New York *Sun*, January 14, 1883, p. 3.

84. Royal Cortissoz, *The Life of Whitelaw Reid* (New York: 1921), vol. 1, p. 231.

85. *Art Amateur* (December 1887), p. 16.

86. Helen Barbara Weinberg, "The Decorative Work of John La Farge," Ph.D. dissertation, Columbia University, Department of Art History and Archaeology, 1972.

87. The panels were painted by P.-V. Galland. They are illustrated in Henri Havard, *L'Oeuvre de P.-V. Galland* (Paris: 1895), p. 211. The research of Mrs. Mary E. Findley supplied this identification.

88. The painting was sold to the Metropolitan Museum of Art circa 1936. Its present location is unknown. A letter of February 13, 1980, from the museum states: "The Metropolitan Museum does not own the painting."

89. *Art Amateur, op. cit.*

90. Bennett Cerf, *At Random* (New York, 1977), pp. 188–91.

91. Lever House, Skidmore, Owings, and Merrill, 1951–1953; Seagram Building, Ludwig Mies van der Rohe, Associate Architect Philip Johnson, 1956–1958; Racquet Club, McKim, Mead & White, 1913–1917; St. Bartholomew's, Bertram G. Goodhue, 1917; Waldorf-Astoria, Schulze and Weaver, 1930–1931.

92. Pennsylvania Station, McKim, Mead & White, 1906–1910; Singer Building, Ernest Flagg, 1907; Metropolitan Opera House, Josiah Cleveland Cady (1881–1883).

93. General Electric Building, Schulze and Weaver, 1931.

94. World Trade Center, Minuro Yamasaki, 1962–1977; Pan Am Building, Pietro Belluschi and Walter Gropius, 1963; General Motors Building, Edward Durell Stone, 1968; Citicorp Center, Hugh Stubbins, 1978.

95. Norman Marcus, Esq., "Villard Preserv'd: Or, Zoning for Landmarks in the Central Business District," vol. 44, *Brooklyn Law Review*, vol. 1 (1977).

Other basic research sources used for the documentation of facts in this book are as follows: New York City Department of Buildings; New York County Register's Office; New York City (Manhattan) Municipal Archives and Record Center; the McKim, Mead & White Collection of The New-York Historical Society; the Charles Platt Collection of the Avery Architectural and Fine Arts Library of Columbia University; the Villard Papers in the Houghton Library of Harvard University; and *The Architecture of McKim, Mead & White, 1870–1920: A Building List* by Leland M. Roth, New York and London, 1978.

Illustration Sources

Page 16, left: Moses King, editor, *King's Handbook of New York City* (New York, 1893).

Page 20, top: Fanny Garrison Villard, *Memoirs of Henry Villard* (Boston and New York, 1904).

Page 31: Dr. Carl Wolff and Dr. Rudolf Jung, *Die Baudenkmaler in Frankfurt am Main* (Frankfort, 1898).

Page 25, below: E. P. Belden, *New York: Past, Present and Future* (New York, 1849).

Pages 26; 62; 116, above: The Architectural Record, Great American Architects Series, 1895–1899.

Page 28, top: John Gilmary Shea, *The Catholic Churches of New York City* (New York, 1878).

Page 32, above: Villas on the Hudson (New York, 1867).

Page 36: Charles Moore, *The Life and Times of Charles Follen McKim* (Boston and New York, 1929).

Page 39, above: Portland, Oregon, Illustrated (Portland, 1892).

Page 39, below: West Shore, April 1882.

Page 40, bottom left: The Architectural Record, Vol. 66, 1929.

Pages 50–51: Edward B. Watson, *New York Then and Now* (New York, 1976).

Page 54: A Monograph of the Works of McKim, Mead & White, 1879–1915 (New York, 1915).

Page 65, above: Earl Shinn (Edward Strahan), *Mr. Vanderbilt's House and Collection* (Japan Edition, Philadelphia, n.d.).

Pages 65, below; 66, below; 69, left; 70, above; 75, below; 77, top; 78–79; 83: Artistic Houses (New York, 1883–1884), courtesy Steven Zane.

Page 69, above right: Homer Saint-Gaudens, *The Reminiscences of Augustus Saint-Gaudens* (New York, 1913).

Pages 108–109: The Architect, August 1926.

Page 116, above, right: H. Havard, *L'Oeuvre de P.-V. Galland* (Paris, 1895).

Page 122, right: Edwin H. Blashfield, *Mural Painting in America* (New York, 1913).

Drawings of architectural details used as decorations for chapter openings: courtesy of Emery Roth & Sons.

Index

(Figures in italics indicate illustrations)

Abbey, Edwin Austin, 117, 123
Abbott, Samuel A. B., 38
Adams, Adoniram Judson, 59
Adams, Edward Dean, 58-60, 87, *89*, 105, 110; house of, 18, *54*, 59, 89–96, 99, 101, *111*, 127, *130*, *135*, 139; *see also* Michalis, Mr. and Mrs. Clarence Gaylor
Adams, Mrs. Edward Dean, *91*
Adams, George H., 59
Adams, Harriet Lincoln Norton, 60
Age of Innocence, The (Wharton), 17
Allard (French firm), 35
Archdiocese of New York, and Villard complex, 117, 126–28, 132, 133
Armstrong, David Maitland, 64
Arthur, Chester A., 58
Arthur, Duke of Connaught, 123
Astor, Caroline Schermerhorn, 47
Astor, John Jacob, Jr., 14
Atheneum (Philadelphia), 47
Atwood, Charles B., 18, 21, 46, 47, *48*

Babb, Cook & Willard, 60, 110, 128, *129*
Babb, George Fletcher, 34, 37, 41, 42, 99, 110, 141
Bacon, Francis, 68, 80, 90
Baker, George F., 63
Banta, John, 87
Barney, C. T., house of, 110
Barry, Charles, 17, 47
Belmont, Oliver Perry Hazard, 47
Beman, Solon S., 58
Bigelow, William A., 46
Bigelow, William B., 34, 35, 37
Billings, Frederick, 23, 58
Bitter, Karl, 59
Blum, Robert, 37
Boston Public Library, 38, 41, *43*, 117
Bramante, Donato, 37
Breck, George W., *122*, 123
Brimmer, Martin, house of, 37
Brown, John, 33
Buckhout, Isaac C., 23
Burges, William, 37
Burke, J. E., 33
Butler, Prescott Hall, 42

Cabus, Joseph, 34, 68
Campbell, Helen Fahnestock, 90; *see also* Hubbard, Helen Fahnestock Campbell
"Cantoria," 74, *75*
Capital Cities Communications, Inc., and Villard complex, 127, 128, *129*, 132, *138*, 139
Cardinal Farley Building, 128
Cardinal Hayes Building, 128
Carman, Richard F., 47
Carnegie, Andrew, 136
Cathedral of Florence, "Cantoria" from, 74, *75*
Cathedral Girls' High School, 132
Cathedral of Salamanca, 35
Catholic Center, 132
Catholic Female Orphan Asylum, 24, *27*
Catholic Male Orphan Asylum, 24
Century Association building, 41, *43*

Cerf, Bennett, 125, 127
Church of Our Lady of Lourdes, *28*
Church of St. John the Evangelist, 24, *28*, 30
Clark, Edward S., 18
Cleveland, Mrs. Grover, *69*
Cloth Hall (Belgium), 36
Cochran, Samuel, 33
Cochran, Thomas, 33
Colford Jones Block, 17, *19*
Colling, J. K., 37
Colonnade Row, 14, *15*
Columbia College, 23, 24, *26*, 30
Cook, Clarence, 113
Covent Garden (London), 13
Cox, Kenyon, *41*
Croton Reservoir, *15*

Dakota apartment house, 17–18
Davis, Alexander Jackson, 14, *15*, 17
Delano, William Adams, 11
Dewing, Thomas W., 37, *41*
Duane & Woodward, 36
Dunedin (Dobbs Ferry house), 33

Edifices de Rome moderne (Letarouilly), 37
Edis, R. W., 37
Edison, Thomas, 23
Edward Albert, Prince of Wales, 123
Ellin & Kitson, 47, 64
Emery Roth & Sons, 133, 136, 137
Endicott, William, Jr., 59

Fahnestock, Clarence, *101*, 105
Fahnestock, Gibson, house of, 110, 128
Fahnestock, Harris C., 34, 89, 105; house of, 18, *27*, 41, *54*, 59, 60, 90, 99–104, 110, 125, 127, *135*; *see also* Random House, Inc.
Fahnestock, Julia Strong Goetchius, 105
Fahnestock, Margaret McKinley, 60, 99
Fahnestock, William, houses of, 18, *27*, *54*, 59, 60, 90, *100*, 101, 105–109, 125, 127, *135*, 139; *see also* Random House, Inc.
Fifth Avenue Hotel, 47, *50*, 52
Flatiron Building, 52
Fosdick, James, 90, 92

Gaisman, Henry J., 132
Galland, P.-V., *126*, 142
Gambrill & Richardson, 34
Garrison, Fanny (Helen Frances), *see* Villard, Fanny Garrison
Garrison, Wendell P., 33
Garrison, William Lloyd, 22, 33
Geer, Seth, 14
Gilbert, Cass, 38
Gilder, Richard Watson, 37, *41*, 60
Glenham Hotel (now Albert Building), *50*, 52
Goelet, Robert, 10, 64
Gould, Jay, 18, 21, 22
Grand Army Plaza, *16*
Grant, Ulysses S., 34, 58, 60
Greeley, Horace, 113

Haight, Charles Coolidge, 23, *26*, 61, 128
Hamilton Hall (Columbia College), *26*
Hardenbergh, Henry J., 18
Harding, Ann, 125
Harrison, Benjamin, 113
Haughwout store, 52
Hay, John, 117
Hay-Adams house (Washington, D.C.), 117
Helmsley, Harry B., 132, 133, 136, 137
Herter, Christian, 63
Herter Brothers, 46, 47, 63, 80
Higgins, George, 17
Hilgard, Ferdinand Heinrich Gustav, family home of, *20*
Hill, Adam S., 22
Hitchcock, Henry-Russell, 10, 52
Hoadly, George and Mary P., house of, 61
Holiday (film), 125
Holladay, Ben, 113
Holland, Josiah G., 60
Holmes, Artemas H., 55, 58–61; house of, 18, *54*, 86–89, 90, 127, 128, *135*, 139
Holmes, Lillian, 89
House of Mansions, *15*, 17
Hubbard, Helen Fahnestock Campbell, 110, *111*, 127; *see also* Campbell, Helen Fahnestock
Hubbard, John, 110
Hunt, Richard Morris, 18, 34, 37, 47, *49*

Idlehour (Vanderbilt country house), 47
India House (originally Hanover Bank), 47
ITT tower, 131

Jones, Inigo, 13
Jones, Mary Mason, *16*, 17, 46
Jones, Rebecca, 17

Kahn, Louis, 10
Kendall, William M., 42, 123
Kennedy, Joseph P., 125, 127
Koerner, Gustav, 22
Kramer, Ellen, 17

La Farge, John, 34, 35, *41*, 68, *70*, *114*, 117
La Grange Terrace, *see* Colonnade Row
Lady Chapel, 18, *28*, 30, 53, *96*
Lathrop, Francis, 34, 37, 64, 74
Le Roy Place, *12*, 13
Letarouilly, P.-M., 37, 52, 53
Lever House, 131
Lienau, Detlef, 17, *19*
Lincoln, Abraham, 22
Lindsay, John V., 131
Lobdell, Mrs. Leighton (Ruth Adams), 89, *91*
Longworth, Nicholas and Alice Roosevelt, 123
Luce, Clarence, 36

Marble Row, *16*, 17, 46
Marcus, Norman, 136

Martiny, Philip, *41*
Mathews, Charles Thompson, 30, *96*
Matthews, Brander, *41*
McGrath, Kevin, 136
McKim, Charles Follen, 11, 33–38, 41, 42, 45, 47, 117, 123
McKim, James Miller, 33, 35, 60
McKim, Lucy, 33
McKim and Mead, 37
McKim, Mead & Bigelow, 34, 69
McKim, Mead & White, 10–11, 17, 18, 24, *32*, 34–36, 38, *39*, 41, *43*, *44*, 45, 52, 54, 55, 60, 68, 69, 74, 83, 87, 89, 90, 99–103, 105, *109*, 110, 113, 117, *120*, 123, 128, *130*, 137
McKinley, William, 113
McMahon, James J., 24
Mead, Larkin Goldsmith, 34
Mead, William Rutherford, 11, 34, 35, 36, 59
Mellon, Paul, 10
Metropolitan Museum of Art, 137, 141
Michalis, Mr. and Mrs. Clarence Gaylor, and Adams house, 90, 92, *94*, *96*, 101, *111*, *135*
Millet, Francis, *41*
Mills, Darius Ogden, 113
Miner, Dorothy, 136
Mitchell, Edward, house of, 61
Mook, Robert, *16*, 17
Morgan, Edwin D., 14
Morgan, J. Pierpont, 10, 11, 18, 59, 60
Municipal Art Society, *138*, 139

New Weston Hotel, 131
New York Central Office Building (now Helmsley Building), 131
New York City Landmarks Preservation Commission, 131–32, 134, 136, 137
New York City Planning Commission, 136
New York Crystal Palace, 52
New York & Harlem Railroad, 24, 25
New York Institute for the Instruction of the Deaf and Dumb, 23, 25
New York Public Library, *15*, 17
Newcomb, H. Victor, 63
Notman, John, 47

Oakes, Thomas Fletcher, 55, 59
Ophir Hall (Ophir Farm), 74, 80, 113, 116, 117, 123

Page, J. Augustus, 24
Palace, The, 90, 110, 134, 137, *138*
Palazzo Cancelleria, 37, *40*, 52
Palazzo Farnese, 37, 52, 53
Pasquali and Aeschlimann, 64
Peabody, Robert S., 33–34
Peabody and Stearns, 37
Pearson, Isaac G., 13
Pei, I. M., 10
Pershing, John J., 123
Peruzzi, Baldassore, 53
Phoenix, Phillips and Lloyd, 110
Platt, Charles, 105, *106*, 107, *109*, 139
Portland House (Oregon), 36, 39

Portland Terminal Station (Oregon), design for, 36, *39*
Post, George Browne, 18, 21, 46, 49, 68
Pullman, George M., 59

Random House, Inc., 125, 127
Reid, Elisabeth Mills and Whitelaw, *112;* and Holmes house, 87; and Ophir Hall, *116,* 117, 123; and Villard house, 58–61, 74, 80, 83, 101, 113–23, 127, 128, *130,* 133, 139
Rensselaer, Mariana Griswold van, 38
Renwick, James, 24, *28*, 30, *96*
Restell, Mme. (Ann Lohman), 24, *27*
Rhodes, James, 136
Richardson, H. H. (Henry Hobson), 34, 35, 45, 68, 80, 99, 117
Robbia, Luca della, 74, 75
Rockefeller Center, *96*
Rohallion (Adams country home), 89, 90, *91*
Rossellino, Antonio, 68
Roth, Richard, Jr., 137
Row, The (Washington Square North), 12, *14*

Saint-Gaudens, Augustus, 34, 37, *41*, 42, 64, 68, 69, 73, 74, 77–80, 90, 123, 133, 139
Saint-Gaudens, Louis, 37, 64
St. John's Church, 132
St. Luke's Hospital, 24
St. Patrick's Cathedral, 18, 23, 24, *26*, *28*, 53, *96*, *125*
St. Thomas Church, 68
Sangallo, Antonio da, 53
Schurz, Carl, 58, 59
Scott, George Gilbert, 36
Scribner, Charles, 60
Seagram Building, 131
Shaw, Richard Norman, 35
Shepard, Mrs. Elliott, house of, *19*
Sherman, Watts (Newport house), 35
Shopsin, William C., 133
Sitting Bull (Sioux chief), 58
Sloane, Mrs. William D., house of, *19*
Smith, Alfred E., 123
Smith, Roswell, house of, 18, *54*, 60, 99, 101, 110–11, 127, 128, *129*, *130*, *135*, 139
Snook, John B., 18, 21, 23, 24, 46, 47, *48*, 52, 141
Society for Decorative Arts, 68
Spellman, Francis Cardinal, 127, 139
Stewart, A. T., house, 46; store, 47
Stokes, Henry, 59
Stokes, Lillian, 59
Stratton, Sidney V., 34
Sturgis, John, 37
Sturgis, Russell, 34

Taft, William Howard, 123
Terry, Ellen, 38
Thomas, Griffith, 47, *50*, 52
Thomas, Lowell, 128, *129*
Thomas, Theodore, 37
Thompson, Frederick F., 69
Thorwood (Villard home in Dobbs Ferry), *32*, 33, 34
Thouvard, Louis, 117, *120*
Thurn and Taxis, Palace of the

Princes of, 30–31
Tiffany, Charles L., 10; house of, 17, *44*, 45, 46
Tiffany, Louis Comfort, *44*, 45, 68, *70*
Tilden, Samuel J., 18
Trench and Snook, 47
Trinity Church (Boston), 34, 35, 68, 117
Tucker, John, 59, 87

Union Club building, 47, *50*
Upjohn, Richard Michael, 68
Urban Center, 139

Vanderbilt, Alva Smith, 47
Vanderbilt, Cornelius, 23, 47; house of, *16*, 18, 21, 46
Vanderbilt, Cornelius, II, house of, 46, 49, 68, 69
Vanderbilt, Cornelius, III, Mr. and Mrs., 123
Vanderbilt, Cornelius Jeremiah, 46
Vanderbilt, William Henry, 24; houses of, 18, *19*, 21, 23, 46–47, *48*, 52, 63, *65*, 69, 123
Vanderbilt, William Kissam, 46; house of, 18, *19*, 21, 47, *48*, 49
Vanderbilt houses (interiors), 64
Vaux & Redford, 18
Victoria, Queen of England, 113
Villa Farnesina, 53
Villard, Fanny Garrison, 22, 33, 34, 61, 80
Villard, Henry, 11, *20*, *57*; birth of, 21; death of, 59; early years, 21–22; home in Dobbs Ferry, *32*, 33, 34; house of, 18, *54*, 55, 63–67, 69, *70*, 73, 75, 77–85, 90, 99, 110, 117; buys land for complex, 24; plan for complex, 30; as railroad tycoon, 22–23, 58; *see also* Reid, Elisabeth Mills *and* Reid, Whitelaw
Villard, Oswald Garrison, 24, 30
Voorhees, Walker, Foley, & Smith, 127

Wagner, Robert, 131
Walker, C. Howard, 37, 42
Walters, Henry, 11
Wanamaker, John and Mary Brown, 87
Warburton, Barclay H. and Mary, 87
Ward, Lady, 123
Weinberg, Barbara Helen, 117
Weir, Julian Alden, *41*
Wells, Joseph Morrill, 11, 36–37, 38, *40*, 41, 42, *43*, 45, 52, 53, 75, 99
Wharton, Edith, 17
Wheeler, Candace, 68
Whidden & Lewis, 36, *39*
White, Horace, 22, 59
White, Richard Grant, 35
White, Stanford, 11, 34–38, 41–45, 68, 78–80, 90, 99, *114*, *116*, 117, 123, 133
Whitney, W. C., 10
Winslow, Mrs. John G. (Helen Louise Michalis), 92
Women's Hospital of the State of New York, 24
World's Columbian Exposition, 46

Yale Center for British Studies, 10

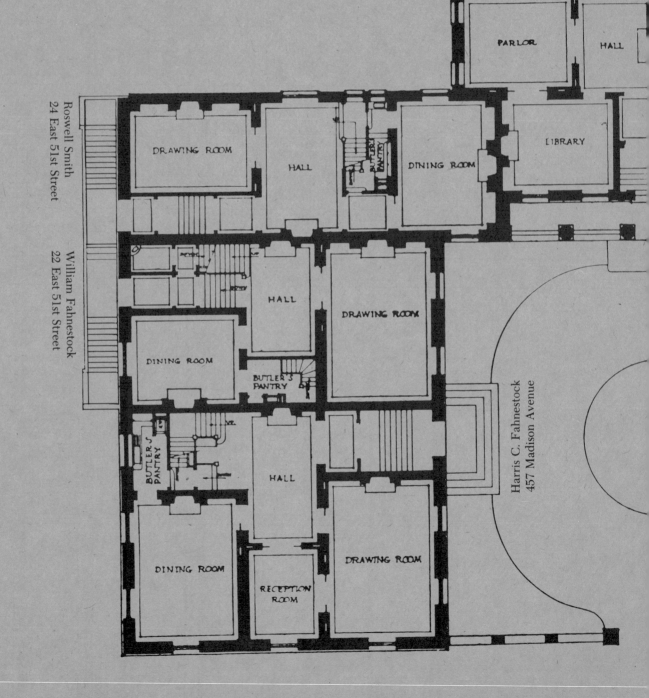

Edward Dean Adams
455 Madison Avenue

DINING ROOM

PARLOR

HALL

LIBRARY

DRAWING ROOM

HALL

BUTLER'S PANTRY

DINING ROOM

HALL

DRAWING ROOM

DINING ROOM

BUTLER'S PANTRY

HALL

BUTLER'S PANTRY

DINING ROOM

RECEPTION ROOM

DRAWING ROOM

Roswell Smith
24 East 51st Street

William Fahnestock
22 East 51st Street

Harris C. Fahnestock
457 Madison Avenue